Amazon FBA

Lessons From
$20,000,000 In 2018

Your Playbook To Building A
$10,000/Month Passive
Income Or Your eCommerce
Empire... You Decide

Sam JT

3

Introduction

Before you devour this book, I want you to be very aware of a few things. This is most likely going to be hard to read. Why do I say that? It's almost 100% actionable content. I know stories are great and engage the reader, but I'll be really honest... I'm a terrible writer so I didn't want you to have to suffer more than you need to!

Here is my recommendation on how to actually read and use this book for maximum efficiency. Go through it all without doing anything. Simply read the material, take a few notes and really take in the material. Make sure you understand it. More importantly, make sure you understand WHY you need to do those things.

Second step for maximum efficiency is read it again but this time much slower. For example, read the product research chapter and as you're reading focus on DOING. Take action on the material in this book. This is the ONLY way you will see results.

This book has all you will need to:
- Learn the fundamentals of Amazon FBA
- Decide how you want to go about selling on FBA
- Figure out what kind of products you will end up selling
- Helpful tips to find the best suppliers
- How to navigate the confusing world of shipping
- What you need to do to create an amazing listing
- Introduction to social media and the steps you should take to build your own list

- Launch your products... what matters more and a few techniques
- Introduction to Amazon PPC and how to optimize your campaigns
- A few really cool bonuses along the way
- And more!

Two more really important things. First, if you have any questions while you're reading this book or building your business and want me to personally answer you, go to http://pixelfy.me/FBGroup and I'll happily welcome you to be a part of our awesome community.

Last thing, download your resource PDF before you start reading. I will refer to a lot of the videos and templates that are inside of it. It's incredibly valuable. Get it at http://pixelfy.me/BookResources

There are a lot of lessons learned from over $20,000,000 in sales in 2018 in various markets such as Europe, USA, and Canada in this book. I hope they are as helpful to you as they've been to hundreds of others!

You can also check out the virtual summit I did with 21 other Amazon experts at http://pixelfy.me/Summit

Chapter 1 - Amazon Fundamentals

Before we get into the nitty gritty, I want to make sure that we're all on the same page. I'll be using a lot of terms specific to Amazon seller and abbreviations in this book. This way, it'll be much easier for you to follow along and to come back to this section if there is anything you're not sure about. I'll also be covering a little bit about mindset and productivity at the end of this chapter. While this is not a self-development book, it's 100% part of the journey to building your own empire.

Terminology

Seller Central - https://sellercentral.amazon.com/
- This is where everything takes place. From adding your bank account, modifying your products to advertising on Amazon. If you aren't familiar with it, take time to browse through all the different pages on Seller Central to make sure that you get familiar with it before going any further.

Fulfilled by Amazon (FBA)
- Amazon handles preparation
- Amazon handles storage
- Amazon handles postage and shipping
- Amazon handles some of the customer service (you will want to do this as much as possible, and I will explain why later)

Merchant Fulfilled (MFN)
- You handle preparation
- You handle storage
- You handle postage and shipping
- You handle customer service

ASIN – Amazon Standard Identity Number
- A value that will be assigned to your product when it is created

SKU
- You will either name your product (however you want, ideally to make it easier for you in the long run when you have a lot of products). If you don't name it, then Amazon will assign random letters and numbers to it for you.
- They are used within Seller Central.

Fulfillment Network Stock Keeping Unit – FNSKU
- A number/barcode that you will print on your packaging. It will be scanned by Amazon when they receive the product.
- It will also contain the Name of the product and the condition of your product.

Fulfillment Fees (FBA Fees)
- The fees charged by Amazon for picking and packing your products and then shipping it directly to your customers. Will be very important to know when calculating your profits before sourcing.

Referral Fees

- This will vary based on the categories, but most of the categories will have a 15% fee. This 15% is based on the price you sold the item for. If you sell your item for $10, you will get charged a referral fee of $1.50.

Best Seller Ranking (BSR)

- How often does an item sell relative to others in the same category?
- A BSR of 1 means you are the most sold in that particular category
- Every category is different. Being the best seller in one category or sub-category does not mean you will sell as much. The competition and sales volume will vary based on the category.
- I don't use it to make decisions, but it is good to know how it works

A9 Algorithm

- It is an algorithm that calculates where your product will show up in the search page results for your different keywords. A lot of factors are factored such as sales velocity, conversion rate, click-through rates, and much more. Don't worry; this will also be covered later!

Indexing

- Indexing refers to whether or not the keywords that are in your title, bullet points, description, and backend will rank for your product.
- What I mean by that is if you're selling a yoga mat, you would want to be indexed for the keyword "yoga mat." It means that when people are

searching for "yoga mat" on Amazon, your listing will show up in the search results.

- If people were to search for "car battery," your yoga mat will not be appearing because it will not index for this keyword.
- A simple way to determine if your ASIN is indexed for a keyword or not is by searching for "ASIN keyword."
    - You will replace ASIN with your actual ASIN and keyword by the keyword you want to verify without including the "."

Your first product – What to expect

Regarding the budget, you will have to consider the following:

- Cost of Goods Sold (COGS) – This is the cost of 1 unit of your product. I will refer to this often. You will need to have a budget allowed for COGS x # of units you will purchase (usually minimum 500). You should have a budget of a minimum of $2,000 for this.
- Customs Bond, Duties and Taxes – Related to shipping. Your freight forwarder will be able to help you with that. I will expand on what all the terms mean in the Shipping module.
- Photography – It is crucial to invest in AMAZING photos. It will usually end up costing $600+ to have 7+ amazing photos done.
- Packaging design – A good packaging will increase the perceived value of your product and can be very important. This will usually cost minimum $100.

- Pay Per Click (PPC) Budget – The PPC cost can be taken from your credit card or directly from your Amazon's balance.
- Lawyers (if applicable)
- Tools (when starting, I would only suggest getting a product research tool as I will discuss in the product research module)
    - Product research – Those tools can be helpful to find products faster and use the data they provide to make better sourcing decisions.
    - Profitability tools – Keeping track of all the fees you are incurring to make sure you are profitable.
    - Keywords – It will help you find which keywords to target, how many searches there are for those keywords, what rank you are for any particular keywords.
    - Advertising – Help you manage all your Amazon PPC campaigns

Financials Metrics

Revenue (also referred to as sales and top line)
- The amount you generated in sales for a certain period. This isn't as important as your actual bottom line; which is the profit you will be taking home after all expenses and costs are subtracted.

Cost of Goods Sold (COGS or I will refer to it as Landed COGS)
- The per unit cost of your product including all expenses. This means that your COGS will include:
    - Cost of the product

- o Shipping
- o Packaging
- o Preparation & Labeling

Net Profit
- This is the final dollar amount that you will receive. Total Revenue – COGS
- In our case, we will also subtract all other Amazon fees from the amount above

Gross Profit Margin (also known as gross margin)
- Gross Profit Margin = (Revenue – COGS) / Revenue
- Some people will include more expenses in this calculation than others.

Return on Investment
- ROI = Net profit / COGS
- If you ROI is 100%, it means that for each 1$ you would invest in the business, you would get another 1$ back.
- This will affect your ability to grow, your cash flows.
- Usually, the higher the ROI will be better. I will go into more details later

Inventory Turnover
- This indicates how fast you turn over (sell) all of your inventory. The faster you sell your inventory means that you will get your investment + profit back and you can reinvest into more inventory and keep growing.
- Some people using this metric to say "My inventory turnover is 4 months" which means that they usually sell all of their inventory every 4 months.

- Others will say "My inventory turnover for the year was 3". This means that over a 1-year period, they turned over their inventory a total of 3 times (or every 4 months).
- The formula is Inventory Turnover = COGS / Average Inventory (for the period you are calculating the inventory turnover for)

Cash Flow
- As you will grow, this will become your most important metric. This is mostly the Cash coming in vs. cash going out.

It is tricky because you can be profitable and yet still have negative cash flows. One example would be that your products have profitable margins, but you are not turning your inventory over fast enough, and you have other costs to pay such as your warehouse rent, employees, software, etc.

Mindset

There are a few key concepts that I try to live by. I think they've served me well and I'm sharing them with you in the hopes that they help you.

It doesn't have to be hard... We tend to unconsciously make things a lot harder than they should be. We're programmed to look for the complex solution because it "must be better" than the simple one. Usually, the simplest solution will be 90-95% perfect and it will be very easy to implement and move on. The complex solution might be 99% perfect, but it could be incredibly hard to implement and use on a daily basis. It's not worth the trouble.

An abundance mindset... There are more than enough opportunities for every single one of you... and more!

Urgency... Get things done RIGHT NOW. Don't delay what you can do now. Even, and especially, if you don't feel like doing it at that moment.

Consistency is key... Motivation is great and all but consistent work every single day will produce the results you're looking for.

No one cares how you feel... It's normal and expected to have your inner voice say "I don't feel like doing this". Acknowledge it and do it anyways. There are no secrets. You MUST do the things you KNOW are crucial no matter how you feel about doing them. Well... maybe that's the secret?

Productivity

We've all had times where we did more work in 1 hour than we normal do in 3-4 hours. That's the power of focus. I do a few simple things every day that make a huge difference. I used to dismiss the exact same things that I'm going to share because I was "different". So please, don't think this doesn't apply to you. It does. It really does. Here are a few things that I do:

Prepare and plan my day the day before. I like to plan 2-3 days ahead at least, but having 1 day planned in advanced works fine. I mean detailed planning. What you will do every 15-30 minutes. I was so surprised how much I actually got done using that simple system. I put everything in my Gmail calendar. It takes a few minutes to do but saves so much time. I never ask myself "what should I do now?". I know exactly what I have to do and I do it. Even when I don't feel like it.

I also use a color system to mark my calendar items as green when they're done and red when something came up or I didn't have time to finish it within the allocated time. This way I know if I missed something for the next day.

Diet and exercise. How shocking right? Go workout or walk at least one a day. It is so refreshing. It's a fantastic time to think or learn new things using podcasts or audiobooks.

Drink a lot of water. I won't advise a certain quantity of water to drink because that varies a lot depending on your weight and physical activity during that day. Just always have a glass of water nearby and drink frequently. Also, drink 500ml of water within the first 5 minutes of waking up. You probably won't believe me until you've done it, but it wakes you up really well. We get really dehydrated during our sleep and this does wonders.

Pomodoro technique. Use an app like Focus Keeper (on iPhone). It will allow you to focus short periods of 20-25 minutes on your work. Then take a small break of 5 minutes to walk around a little bit, breathe and drink water. Then, focus again. Repeat the cycle 4 times and take a longer break. If you want more information, simply google the Pomodoro technique. Give it a shot.

Chapter 2 - Product Research

Product selection is incredibly important. Whether you decide to go with method #1 or #2, it will be crucial to your success. If your product selection is good, it will make most of what will be covered in the next chapters much easier.

There are a few basic concepts you should be aware of before starting your product research:

- **Don't look for the perfect product.** There is no such thing as a perfect product. If you approach this step with the mentality that you're only looking for home run products, you will never be satisfied with the products you're finding. It will make you feel desperate and feel like there are no good opportunities left on Amazon. Rest assured, the playing field is still wide open!
- **Leave your negative beliefs and biases at the door.** Go into your product research with an open mind. Don't judge a product based on what it looks like. Sometimes we'll tend to ignore products just because we don't know what it is or it looks weird. Keep an open mind and don't leave stones unturned.
- **Be patient.** Do not expect to find your first product within 1 hour. Yes, it can happen, but it's very unlikely. Be aggressively patient. Spend as much time as it takes for you to find at least 10 solid product ideas before investigating each of them in

more details. It doesn't matter if it takes you two weeks to do it, make sure it's done right.

- **Be data-driven.** You will look at the products without any bias. The data will guide your selection. I will expand on this later and show you which type of criteria to look for.
- **Take the plunge.** Do not let fear be in control of your decisions. That's why it's important to be data-driven. What I will teach you will give you the tools you need to be confident and overcome the fear.

Before going into great details, there are two distinct ways to look for products.

1. Use different criteria such as price, reviews, and sales to find promising products; or
2. Find a market and decide WHO you want to serve instead of WHAT to sell.

1st Method – Products that are not related

Using the 1st way, you will go on Jungle Scout, Viral Launch, Helium10 or whatever else website there is and use the pre-determined criteria to find products to source. This method is a lot easier and requires less deep thinking and planning. This is what almost everyone does. It's easier to get started in the short term, but it's harder in the long term. There are some pros and cons for both.

Pros – It requires less work to get started. Although, I don't necessarily think this is a best pro because it means lower barrier to entry but I put it there anyway.

Cons – You will need to "start over again" every time you want to launch a new product. Harder to build a list of repeat customers. Much harder to build a sellable company that way. You're almost required to provide steep discounts when you're launching products. We'll discuss the launch methodologies in Chapter 8.

I want to add that this doesn't mean that you can't or shouldn't do it that way. You can still make a lot of money. I know plenty of people who are doing very well doing selling on Amazon using this method. I feel like it is a very "dangerous" approach. The way I see it is with the number of sellers looking for products the same way (and you can't forget those nice Chinese sellers that don't play by the rules), the products you are selling are bound to have an influx of sellers and if you don't have a brand, a strong Unique Selling Proposition, it is likely that your sales will eventually drop. So will the profit margins (that's what has been happening to most sellers if you look at the last 3 years +).

2nd Method – Building a brand

The 2nd way is different. You target a certain type of people. Think of it as "people who ...". An example could be to target people who <u>do yoga</u>. Keep in mind, I don't recommend this particular niche, but you get the point. Now, how would you find such niches? There are many ways to do that.

- Use product research software a little bit differently. You won't need to rely as much on the same criteria as you would have with the 1st method. Therefore, you could, if you wanted to, cast a bigger nest and get more ideas using the different product research software. **I mean not focus only on products or markets with extremely low reviews...**

- Think of activities you do, hobbies you have, things you care about. Ask your friend and entourage about their activities, hobbies, what they care about...
- Listen to everyone around you. We're always complaining about how we wish that ABC product did a specific thing. How that product would be better if it had Y... While you may not use those exact ideas, it can help you to look into that product and see that the niche has plenty of great product opportunities.

With the 2nd method, the goal is to find your niche and then it'll be easier for you to come up with 3 to 5 products to release. What makes it so much better is that you will build an audience on Facebook and Instagram while you're sourcing the product. By the time your product arrives at Amazon (~90 days), you will have a Facebook page/group and an email list which you will use to drive traffic to your Amazon listing without having to give huge discounts. What's EVEN better, is that you can contact your list again to get in touch with who bought and follow up with them so they leave a review. Since they're already following you, they'll be much more receptive to your requests and you'll get reviews a lot faster.

Pros – You end up having more control over your customers since you're building an email list of a target market. It will be easier rank faster since you will send outside traffic to Amazon that will convert well. You will do less or no discounted launches. You will build a sellable company. It is easier to grow much faster using this method because of repeat customers and word of mouth. It is also so much easier to get reviews!

Cons – It's scarier to get started this way because it seems like there are so many more steps involved. It requires you to get out of your comfort zone more. You need to learn to use Social Media to a certain extent until you can outsource it.

Where to sell

Where should you start selling first? If you live in Canada, start with the United States. If you're in the United States, sell in the United States. If you're in Europe, sell in Europe. Keep it simple.

While the United States is so much bigger than the European and Canadian market, Europe still has a fantastic potential. It benefits from:
- Less competition
- Higher prices – Most of the time the same item will sell for more EUR than it sells in USD.
- Higher Barrier to entry (VAT, multiple countries, etc...)
  - It's harder to start selling, but it's worth it because it seems like everyone is scared!
- You get access to 5 marketplaces by sending your inventory to one country
- Germany is a great market to sell in. They will tend to pay more for quality (or perceived quality). France is also good and often overlooked. UK is great as well. Italy is decent. Spain is total garbage!

Selling in Europe also requires more work as you must get your listings translated into French, Italian, Spanish & German and you should never use Amazon's automated translating. But overall, I feel it's easier to find a niche that's "wide open" compared to the USA. It doesn't mean that Amazon USA doesn't still have amazing opportunities, because it does.

Helpful criterion to look for

Starting your product research using those tools can still be quite confusing. Here are some of the criterion I recommend you use to find products that you can then further investigate:

- **Sale price**: $15 – $75 – Some go for lower than $15. Although it can work, it will mostly depend on the price you can source your product for and the cost of Amazon Advertising (pay per click). If it is too expensive, it will eat all your margins.
- **Number of units/month**: Minimum 250 (If you're looking at a product that sells for $25, it means that the minimum monthly sales volume would be $5,000)
- **Number of reviews**: Maximum 250 – I don't mind the competition. When you have your own list, it makes so much easier to pierce those markets.
- **Product size**: Don't be scared to go for oversized products. As long as your final profit margins are still healthy.
- **Product Age**: This is not a filter that you will find on the tools you'll be using. If you find a product and/or niche you are interested in; I recommend validating the number of days those products have been selling. You can look at the number of days

the products have been selling using the Keepa extension. If your product doesn't have 100 days of history, the odds that the extension/tools' numbers are correct are very low (not enough history, the possibility of launch occurring).

- **Untouched Niches** – There are great advantages to getting into an underdeveloped niche (less competition). You will be able to rank much faster and easier for your main keywords. You'll be able to control a bigger share of a (usually smaller) market. As long as it respects the number of units sold per month, you will be fine with this approach. _You have to be careful though. Everyone is using the same criterion to find products. It means that this niche will most likely get inundated by a lot of products in the next 1-3 months!_

- **Simplify your life** – Especially in the beginning, don't make it harder than it has to be. Stick with:
  - One size (no color/size variations)
  - No complicated moving parts
  - Relatively easy to differentiate your product vs. what is available for sale now

Financial Metrics

- Return on Investment (ROI) of minimum 120% (150%+ preferred)
  - ROI = Landed Product Cost / Net Profit
- Profit Margins over 30%
  - Net Profit / Revenue (sale price in this case)

Analyzing Your Competition

There are a few factors that are important for you to evaluate your competition. This way you'll know how easy or hard it will be for you to dominate your market. Here are the factors:

1. # of reviews – How many reviews do the top competitors have? If everyone on the first page has over 500 reviews, it will be much harder for you to reach and stay on the first page than if the average amount of reviews of the first page is maximum.

   - Less than 250 is ideal.
   - It's also important to look at opportunities for improvement. If the review rating (out of 5 stars) is below 4 stars, then you'll most likely have a lot of opportunities to improve the product and stand out.
   - When you find those listings, you can go through all their 1-2-3 star reviews to find ideas on what to improve.

2. Keywords – Which keyword did you use on Amazon (search bar) to find the competitors? It's crucial that you use the best keywords to see which competitors you will be against. See next section for a more detailed coverage!

3. Who is your competition? – Are you planning to sell a product in a category that is dominated by Amazon or another seller?

4. All the same – Some categories have products that are ALL comparable. Every product could be a substitute for the other, and it would make no difference at all. Stay away from those markets.

5. Listing Quality – Based on a few factors:

   - Do they have HIGH-QUALITY images?

- Are they properly using their title with the right keywords?
- Are their bullet points well crafted? Do they only state short product features or longer bullet points with benefits that solve the pain points of this market?
- Do they have Enhanced Brand Content?
- Do they have a coupon displayed on their listing?
- Are they priced competitively?

6. Listing History – Using Keepa (http://bit.do/keepa)
    - You will see for how long this product has been selling. The older it is, the more you can trust the product research tools.
    - Is it a seasonal product? Sometimes it's obvious and other time it's not.
    - Has the price been fluctuating?
    - What does his review acquisition look like? Has it been increasing alertly fast or at a regular pace? (it now requires a paid version to see the review evolution)

Keywords

I won't go into keyword research just yet. While you're looking for a product on Amazon, you'll be on what we call the search page (the page you land on after typing what you're looking for in Amazon's search bar). You always want to be 100% sure that you're using the main keyword when you're doing that. To find the main keyword, there are a few additional steps you should take:

- Analyze the title – the main keyword(s) will usually be in the first 3-5 words of the listing title.
- Use a keyword research tool (or a Reverse ASIN on the best seller in the category) to make sure that you're using the best keyword. By best keyword, I mean the one that is the most relevant to this product while having the highest possible search volume.

Why is that even important? You want to see what it looks like to be selling on page 1. You don't want to compare yourself with listings that are NOT on page 1 for the HIGHEST search volume keyword that's relevant to your product.

Where to look for product ideas?

Where will you find your product ideas?
- You can find ideas using Jungle Scout, Viral-Launch, or Helium10's Product Research Software. The only downside is that you will be looking at the same results as 10,000s of people.
- If you want to find other ideas, you can look at:
  - Amazon's Best Seller Lists – Dig deep into the sub-categories for good ideas. It is updated hourly so you can browse through it once in a while and find different ideas.
  - Amazon's New Releases – Also updated hourly.
  - Amazon's Movers & Shakers – Biggest gain in sales rank
  - Amazon's Most Wished For

- o Amazon's Gift Ideas
- To find any of the links above, type "Amazon Best Sellers" or "Amazon Movers & Shakers" on google, and you will get the direct link.
- **Seller storefront** – Once you've found an interesting product, click on the listing and look at the seller's storefront. It may help provide you with a lot more ideas of related products if they are building a niche. Or non-related products if they are selling random products.
  - o To find the storefront, look for "Sold by *SELLER NAME* and Fulfilled by Amazon" Click on the seller name and then look for "SELLER NAME Storefront" above the seller's name. If you can't find those, use the search function on your browser (CTRL + F) and look for "Sold by" when you're on the product listing and then "Storefront" when you're on the Seller Profile.
- Also Bought – Customers who bought the product you're currently viewing also bought those other products. This list will appear in the product listing page as well.
- Exploring outside of Amazon – What are you using in your day to day life? Do you have any hobbies? Do your friends have any hobbies that could give you product ideas? Look for opportunities in your daily life and then go on Amazon to validate those products. You can also look at those websites for additional ideas:
  - o Alibaba, Instagram, Etsy, eBay, Wish, Reddit, Forums, Facebook Groups, Kickstarter, Trendhunter, Groupon, Other International Amazon Marketplaces (what

29

is selling well in the US could potentially also work in Europe for example).

- **Think outside of the box**. Do you see anything trending? Is there an increasing demand for a certain product or category? Think about what other products those people will buy resulting from their purchase of that trending product. What other products they could want to use along with that product, etc. This is a similar approach to "selling shovels" to the people during the gold rush.

If you're using Viral launch, look at the keywords section on Market Intelligence, it's much better.

General Tips & Tools

Free Tools

- https://trends.google.com/trends/ (select the region you want to sell i)
  - It's a great way to see how much the demand varies during a year or if the general niche is growing or declining. Use the 5-year period to have a better view.
- https://adwords.google.com/aw/keywordplanner/ideas/new - Google Keyword Planner is also a great way to look at the general demand for different keywords. It's free. You may have to sign up and create an ad to use it though. If that's the case, then create an ad and then pause/archive the ad and you'll be able to use it for free forever.
- When you use tools such as Jungle Scout or Viral Launch, and you think you've found a good product/niche, **make sure that the**

products/competitors already selling have been selling for at least 3 months. If not, then the sales estimates are probably not accurate.

- Using the "Keepa – Amazon Price Tracker" Google Extension (http://bit.do/keepa) to see how your competitors priced their products and how many reviews they received (has it been a slow increase? Did they buy a ton of review? Did they lose a lot of review?)
- Helium10 Google Extension – Product Research (http://bit.do/helium10extension)

Other Paid Tools

- o Take a look at the resources PDF to see exactly which tool I recommend.

What you may want to avoid

- Fad items
- Seasonal items (it's fine, as long as it's not your first product in that niche)
- High liability products (sharp, risk of injuries)
- Complicated to use (Unless you 100% KNOW that it will not be an issue, stay away from products that will confuse the customers when they receive them)
- Electronics – unless you are confident you will be able to find a very high quality supplier and you will work diligently to be sure that everything is inspected before it is shipped from China.

This list should in no means discourage you from selling any of those products (except maybe fads). If you can find a great niche in which you know, you'll be able to solve a problem and provide a quality product, then go for it. You may end up with even less competition.

How to differentiate and add Value to the products

There are so many ways to add value to different products. I will cover the basic ones. The others will vary depending on what kind of product you're selling

- **Bundling** – It's great IF what you're adding with the product makes sense.
    1. You don't want to bundle just for the sake of it. The customer is not dumb and will know that he's usually paying more for your bundle to make sure what you're adding is something that everyone will want along with the main product. **Would this bundle entice the people buying it?** It's not because you think it's cool that it is
    2. Use "Frequently Bought Together" section to get ideas. You can also use a free tool that creates a map of connections based on their "bought together" products. Try it: http://yasiv.com/ - make sure to select "All" before searching and search for the keywords you'd want to target.
    3. ***Try to bundle in a way that doesn't increase the size of your packaging, that's even better!
- **Quantity Packs**
    1. Does it make sense to offer more?

2. Will selling 5 pieces help vs. 4 pieces? You have to research to see if people are asking for more.
3. You're lowering your FBA fees and increasing the perceived value

- **Product Improvements**
    1. You should NEVER buy a product, put your logo on it and sell it. Add massive value. Make it better. It's never been easier to know EXACTLY what the customers want.
    2. Download the "Helium 10" Google Extension and use their free "Review Downloader." http://bit.do/helium10extension to download it.
    3. You will be able to instantly extract all the reviews from a listing directly to a CSV and then search for patterns. It's a much easier and faster way to find what improvements people want on any products.
- **Different Material/Aesthetics**
- **More functionality**
- **Sizing**
    1. Take a product that is oversized and make it fit in standard size. More information on sizes: https://sellercentral.amazon.com/gp/help/external/201105770?language=en-US&ref=mpbc_201119390_cont_2011057 70
- Do not be scared of the competition. Here's why:
    1. Most of the people you're competing against are simply not good. They're not offering the best customer service

possible, they're not providing an additional guarantee, they don't optimize their listings, they're satisfied with being mediocre, they are in love with their products (in a way that makes them biased and impedes their judgment when it comes to improving their product, process, and overall business). You should not aim to do all of this... if ALL of this is your baseline and you're ALWAYS striving to get better, you will not have to worry about what the others are doing.

2. Not having a lot of money to work with is an advantage that can't be bought. It forces you to be creative in a way the bigger corporations don't.

3. You MUST be different. If you're always worried about others, you don't get to focus on what makes you great. The Purple Cow by Seth Godin is a great book you should about this particular subject.

Here are some questions you may want to ask yourself when differentiating your products:

- If the product is more high-end, can I make a less expensive version?
- If the product is "cheaper", can I make a pricier, more "high-end" version?
- If it's larger, can I make a compact version? A travel-friendly version?
- If it's ugly, can I make an aesthetically-pleasing version?

- If it's a product normally used by men/boys, can I make a version that women/girls would use? Or vice versa?
- If it's a product aimed at adults, can I make a child-friendly version? If it's a product aimed at kids, can I market something similar to adults?
- Can I use the product to meet the needs of some niche group, like people who live in warm climates, people who are blind, pet owners, people over age 60, teenagers, people who have large families, those who wear plus-size clothing, etc....
- Can I offer different colors or textures or sizes?
- Can I offer a product that has more than 1 use?

Category-specific Information

Interesting categories that are overlooked
- Industrial & Scientific
- Office Products
- Automotive

For categories requiring approval or restricted products, you can simply type "amazon gated category" and "amazon restricted products" on google and you will find all the up to date information.

Patent & IP

You don't want to be selling a product that's protected by a patent. The seller will enforce the patent, and you will end up not being able to sell this product on Amazon at all. Here are a few things you can do so you don't end up selecting a product that's patented (ps. I'm not a lawyer, and this is not legal advice!):

- Is the product you're looking at completely unique? There are no others like it? You should do more research because the odds that it is patented are high.
  - Check in the listing – even if it says patent pending on the listing you may want to additional research as they may be only trying to scare potential sellers away.
- Product – they are required to show it on the product itself or packaging
- Company website – some will have a section dedicated to IP
- Don't take the word of your supplier; they want to sell more of their products so they may not be upfront about it

Utility Patent – protects the way an article is used and works
Design Patent – protect the way an article looks

Patents may only exist in one country or may be expired. Hence why you need to do the research! To help you, use those resources:

- USPTO.gov
- Google Patents
- IP Lawyer

Get Started Now!

You can use the questions below to also come up with product ideas. Those simple questions will help you to find more than 1 product in the same niche, and you will be able to dominate a single niche. This is more targeted to

Identify your target customer. **Who exactly is this person?**

Where does your target market hang out? (Forum, Facebook Groups, Reddit, etc...)
-   Find at least 5

What pain points does your product solve?
-   Find at least 5

Which other products does your target customer usually buy? Can you use someone else's audience to grow yours (partnerships, affiliate, be creative)?
-   An example of this would be people who do CrossFit. There is a big following who use hand products. Look at that website https://riptskinsystems.com/
    o   I don't know these guys or how well they're doing, but they found a niche and are selling all related products. This gives you an idea of how it could work for you.
    o   They are going after a very specific target market. People who do CrossFit and want/need hand products to take care of the hands before, during and after workouts...

Go to the book resources (http://pixelfy.me/BookResources) at the FREE Training section to get video training on Product Research and Product Sourcing!

Chapter 3 - Product Sourcing

Importing from China or other countries can be tricky, especially when you don't know how the Chinese work for example. Before going deeper, there are a few things to consider when you're dealing with the Chinese suppliers:

- The manufacturers will try to get as much out from you as they possibly can because they expect you to either a second time or in large quantities.
- They are used to have people like you being rude to them. It's so important to build a great relationship with your supplier. Ask them how they are doing, ask simple things instead of going straight to the point. I recommend investing a little bit of time doing this after your first inquiry where they sent you the first batch of information you requested. In the long run, if you do repeat business with them and build a partnership, you will get better quality products, better pricing, better payment terms.
- Don't push too hard for the price. Yes, you can and should always negotiate. But at one point, the Chinese will say yes to lower the price, and they will start dropping the quality of your product and cutting corners, without telling you, so that they can still retain your business.
- OVERCOMMUNICATE. Do Skype calls, send them drawings of what you want, explain in excruciating details. Talk to them through WeChat. Don't take for granted that they will understand. Spend the

extra minute explaining to make sure that they fully understand.

- This goes with the over communicating part. When placing an order, make sure that every detail is specified and agreed upon by both parties. You want to make sure that all your product specifications are detailed in the contract.

Before contacting suppliers

Create a new email address. Don't use your brand name or any information related to your brand. Make it something generic. Once you start sending requests to different suppliers, you will get bombarded by other random suppliers as well. I recommend setting up a Gmail account and using their label features to differentiate between different products as well.

If you need a phone number, you can set up a Google Voice number instead of giving them your real phone number. For the same reason mention above.

Set up a WeChat account on your phone. This is probably the easiest way to discuss with your supplier once you have sent 1-2 messages. They are very responsive, and it will be faster to communicate like this rather than email, especially when there is a lot of back and forth going on.

Do some research. Make sure that you have all the information you need.
- What material you want to use.
- Specific dimensions? Specific weight?
- What packaging you would like.
- The number of units you want to order

- The colors
- Any feedback you found during your product research (mostly what to improve)
- Photos of your competitors if you want to explain what you'd like done for example
- Any certification or restrictions. Do you need a certificate to sell that product? Can your supplier provide it?

Business
- It's better if you already have set up a business with a corporate bank account.
- You can use PayPal for small samples or orders only
- Wire Transfers are the norm once you get comfortable
- Alibaba Trade Assurance works as well, especially when you haven't worked with a supplier before. If you want to get taken seriously, it will be through Wire Transfer.

Terminology of Sourcing

Before you contact suppliers, there are a few terms you should be aware of. The first one is Incoterms which stands for International Commercial Terms. This dictates when the ownership and responsibility are being transferred from the supplier to the buyer. When dealing with suppliers, you will get quoted either EXW or FOB.

EXW (Exworks) – Buyer (you) is responsible for the transportation of the goods from the supplier's warehouse. You will need to contact a forwarder at the country of origin. The pricing will not include any local transportation cost to the airport or port.

FOB (Free on Board) – The supplier is responsible for the transportation of the goods up until the agreed points of destination. If it says "FOB Ningbo," it means that they will transport your items to the port to be shipped by sea. The local (supplier's country) transportation cost is included in the pricing.

When talking with suppliers, I recommend getting all your quotes in FOB to make it simpler for you (and for comparison's sake).

MOQ – Minimum Order Quantity. It's always negotiable. If they don't want to go below their stated MOQ, which is very rare, you can suggest that you would pay a little bit more per unit if they lower the price. Surprisingly, they may only raise the price by $0.05-$0.10, and you can get a much smaller MOQ.

Lead Time – The time between the initiation and completion of a production cycle. They will generally consider initiation when they receive the payment in their bank account, but that depends on your relationship with them. Be careful about the holidays in China and Q4. They will cause delays in your production cycle. You can also ask them if it's working or calendar days. How many days per week do they work? If any holidays are coming up. You should also factor a few extra days (2-3) at the end of the production for the inspection.

Customs Bond – Main purpose is to guarantee the payment of import duties and taxes. You have two choices.

- Continuous bond – Good for 1 year, about $400
- Single-use – one time, usually $65 per entry

Supplier 101

Now onto the basic. When sourcing, most people go to Alibaba.com. This isn't bad in itself, but you want to make sure there are no better options for you out there before. All the sites are pretty much straightforward to us. Other websites that are worth trying:

- www.made-in-china.com *NOT TO BE CONFUSED WITH MADEINCHINA.COM*
- www.hktdc.com
- www.1688.com (this is the equivalent of Alibaba but usually within China)
    - A lot of the supplier you will find on Alibaba will source their products directly from 1688.com and resell to you at a small premium. This is why it may be worth to get a sourcing agent to interact with 1688 suppliers on your behalf when you know exactly what you want.

A few last points about Alibaba.com

- **Gold Suppliers**: This has no real value. It is pretty much a requirement for suppliers to buy this badge on Alibaba now. Sometimes, a business could have a "10 years gold supplier badge," and it could simply be that the old business failed and a new business took over. Take it with a grain of salt.
- **Assessed Suppliers**: If you are considering a supplier, look for their assessment PDF report. It is

the only part of Alibaba's verification system that is of any value.

- **Manufacturer or Trade Company**: As I mentioned earlier, most of the manufacturers will source their products from REAL manufacturers in 1688. Therefore, few of the suppliers on Alibaba.com are REAL manufacturers. One way to verify is with the assessment report and see if the inspection company confirmed their status as a manufacturer and that the report is up to date.
- **Transaction History**: Adds a little bit more credibility if they have 100s of transactions vs. no transaction. But this should not be your only criteria.

If you want to do additional vetting on your manufacturer, you can check if their Postal code matches with their phone area code. (http://www.china.org.cn/english/MATERIAL/120745.htm) You may also want to do a google search of the manufacturer's name.

Find the best suppliers faster

The best way to find suppliers with top quality products in minutes is quite easy. Even more now since JungleScout has released their new "Supplier Search" Tool.

Go to http://pixelfy.me/BookResources to download the resources for this book and you will see the exact template and step-by-step way to do it! (PS. It's in the FREE Training section in the Product Sourcing module)

With the name of the supplier, you can google their name and find how to contact them. Instead of hitting up 10+ random suppliers, you can get about 3 extremely high-quality suppliers in a few minutes.

That's great. **What about if someone else wants to do it to you?** There are a few ways to make sure it doesn't happen. The first way is if your business name is not the same or has no relation with your seller name on Amazon. The second way, which is much safer, is to block it completely from showing up in those lists in the first place. There will be a template in the resources section!

Save money on samples & do a REAL quality test

Hopefully, now that you know exactly where your competitors got their 5-star product, instead of ordering a sample directly from the manufacturer, what you could do is order the product directly from your competitor on Amazon. The reasons behind this are:

- You get the sample faster
- You pay much less for the sample (psst – you can even return the samples after you've tried them to get a refund... this way you literally paid 0$. I won't tell if you don't 😊)
- The manufacturer can't send you their "perfect" product that they keep only for samples. You get a much better sense of the quality of product that way.
- You also get to see your competitor's review acquisition sequence (email, inserts, etc...) and you can learn new things

- If you want to save money, then you can return the sample and get a refund

Once you have the samples, use them and ABUSE them. Drop them, shake them, wash them, etc. Whatever normal usage should be, do that x10. Depending on the type of product you're sourcing, you want to get a feel for the product's toughness, durability, flexibility, ease of use. Lend it to your friends if you can. Do whatever you think you need to to make it endure years' worth of usage within a short period. This is not perfect, but it's much better than just looking at the sample.

Searching on Alibaba

Sometimes the method above doesn't work so that you can search directly on Alibaba. Be aware that you may have to be creative regarding your keywords. Sometimes you will have to try a few different keywords before finding what you're looking for. You can also use the filter feature to only show gold suppliers, assessed suppliers, suppliers with Trade Assurance. You'll also want to avoid any supplier that has "trade" in their name. It means that they are a trading company.

You'll also want to verify what they specialize in. Look at their web catalog (or request that they send it through your email). Usually, they will focus on a certain category or material. Suppliers with similar products to what you're looking for may already have a mold that for it. If they can't make it, you can ask them if they know someone who can!

The price per piece on Alibaba that you will see is almost always inaccurate. I recommend that you contact the supplier directly through the page of the product you're interested in rather than their company page. Provide them with the email you created for that purpose and most of them will reply to this email instead of Alibaba. You will also be able to use the spreadsheet (PLE – Supplier Sourcing) provided to keep track of all the suppliers you contacted and rate them.

At this point, you probably haven't settled on ONE product yet. You will, therefore, be reaching out to multiple suppliers (5-8) for each product. It will be important to use the spreadsheet properly to keep track of everything. I also recommend you use the template in the Annex to reach out to the suppliers.

Ordering Samples on Alibaba (if the method above didn't work out)

For your samples, be prepared to pay $30-60. This is the normal range. It is to cover the express shipping to wherever you want it delivered. That's the cost of doing business. Sometimes, they will quote you $150-200. They are most likely trying to rip you off because they think you won't order from them anyways. The other reason why they would charge that much is that they would create the product for you with your packaging. Like if it were the final product. I don't recommend this.

A few extra tips:
- Ask for a photo or video of the sample before it's sent. Sometimes miscommunication happens, and they won't send you exactly what you needed. This is a great way to avoid those scenarios.

- If there are different versions of the product, ask them all to be sent at the same time.
- Ask for a sample of the packaging (without your design/logo) and catalog to be included.
- Save the tracking numbers in case they don't include a business card (Ask them to include a business card – They usually call it a "name card"). This will be important if you receive too many samples and are struggling to find out which is which.

You will still need to use the same testing standards as I mention in the section above if you order samples through Alibaba.

What quantity should I order?

There are a lot of factors to take into consideration, especially when starting. Here are the most important ones:
- The MOQ you were able to negotiate with your supplier.
- Budget – How much are you willing to invest at this time?
- Competition – How competitive is the niche/product you will be selling in? If your goal is to get at the top of page 1 (hopefully without the use of 90% off giveaways, as you will see later), then you will need to know approximately how many per day the top 3-5 are selling. If they're doing 100/day and you order 1,000, there is realistically no way you will reach page 1 and stay there without running out of stock instantly. I recommend ordering 3 months of inventory based

47

on your approximation of the numbers using a tool like Helium 10.

- More conservative – If you aren't too sure and want to be more conservative, you can always order a fixed amount between 500 – 1000 (I recommend 1000 rather than 500, unless you're in a very low competition market).
- Risk and Reward – It's highly unlikely that you will get stuck with inventory if you follow what I tell you very closely. But it is still business, and there are always risks associated with it. The higher your initial investment, the easier and faster it can be to grow.
- Running out of inventory is one of the worst things that can happen. If you're selling 50 units a day at 5$ profit, you're making $250 a day. If you run out of stock for a month, you're essentially losing out on $7,500 of profit and most likely more as it will take you time to ramp back up your sales velocity to 50 units per day. There are other reasons why running out of stock hurts (product ranking, hijackers), and I will cover them later.

Keep in mind that your inventory (like customer service and a few other things – as I'll cover later) are not expenses. They are INVESTMENTS.

Negotiation tricks

Some of them seem ridiculous, but try them for yourself and see:

1. While you're on a call with the supplier, tell them you have to talk to your boss. Leave for a few minutes and come back and tell them that your

boss gave you a maximum price to pay per unit for example. It doesn't matter that you don't have a boss or you're alone in your home.

2. Using titles like Sourcing Agent or Purchasing Manager to make it seem like you're from a large company.

3. Tell them that you are getting prices from 5 different factories. It will let them know that you have other options.

4. Pitch them against another manufacturer. If you found a good manufacturer and you want to try to lower the price, tell them you have this other one that has a better price. Try to figure out with them why their pricing is higher than their competitor's.

5. Sell them on how big you'll be and how impactful your business will be to them. Maybe you're from a big brand they know so you can tell them you have all the knowledge necessary to make it, etc.

6. Test order – Tell them that you're willing to order 1,000 units now if everything works out great and the product is as good as they claim then you will order 3,000 in a few weeks after the reception of the 1,000 units.

7. Order more. You will have more power to negotiate with them. You can order 5,000 units now and only get 2,000 shipped while they store the 3,000 for you. They will usually not charge you any storage fees, and you will pay less per unit.

8. Always be prepared to walk away. This gives you a lot more power when you know you have other options, and if they're not ready to help you, you'll find someone help who will.

Know your numbers (it's so important that I include it here again)

This is something almost everyone struggles with. We tend to underestimate the expenses for our products and end up with a much smaller profit margin than we initially anticipated. Before sourcing any product, figure out the following:

- Sale Price – How much will you sell it for?
- Cost of goods sold (COGS) – What is your cost to get it produced (+ packaging and inserts)?
- Shipping – How much TOTAL will it cost me (you will see that in the next module)?
- Advertising – Have a budget for PPC already included in your product. The goal is to have your PPC optimized. But this is not always easy or fast to do. Therefore, take into account about **10% of your sale price** as the budget for your PPC. (most people will not take this into account before…)
- FBA Referral Fee – **15% of your sale price**
- FBA Pick & Pack – Use https://sellercentral.amazon.com/gp/help/help.html?itemID=201411300 to figure out what your EXACT fee will be. Read this section carefully and get in touch with Amazon's Customer Support if you're not sure about which category you will fall into. Be careful not to be TOO close to the limits for your size category because the way they calculate it can sometimes make you fall in the next one. The weight of your product will also be important. Take into account that Amazon will add about 0.25 lb to it because of the packaging they will use to ship your product. KNOW the fees

before sourcing, or you will be very surprised with your margins.

- Calculating your Profit Margin and ROI (Return on Investment)
    - Profit Margin (PM) = Profit / Sale Price (Profit is your Sales price – all the fees above)
        - Over 30% considering ALL of those expenses is very good. Aim for that.
    - ROI = Profit / Landed COGS (COGS + TOTAL Shipping)
        - Aim for at least 120%, the higher, the better.

Depending on your Inventory Turnover, you can get away with lower ROI and PM. Your Inventory Turnover is the amount of time you sell and replace your inventory during a certain period. Be careful about your cash flow through. This is a different issue and will not be covered in details as it varies too much from one situation to another. Consider these 2 scenarios:

Scenario 1

You have a profit of $5 on a sales price of $20. Your landed COGS is $4. You end up "turning over" your inventory 3 times during a year (5000 units/order). (PM = 25%, ROI = 125%)

Overall, you invested 5000 units x 3 times x $4 = $60,000
You sold 5000 units x 3 times x $20 = $300,000
Profit = 25% x $300,000 = $75,000

Scenario 2

51

You have a profit of $3.25 on a sales price of $20. Your landed COGS is $4. You end up "turning over" your inventory 5 times during a year (5000 units/order). (PM = 16.25%, ROI = 81.25%)

Overall, you invested 5000 units x 5 times x $4 = $100,000
You sold 5000 units x 5 times x $20 = $500,000
Profit = 16.25% x $500,000 = $81,250

Some people prefer turning their inventory more often at a lower profit; some don't. In this particular example, you would make more profit in Scenario 2, but you would also have used $40,000 more to make $6,250 more. This is why Cash Flow management is important. Do you think you could have accomplished a better ROI than 15.63% (6250/40000) using the additional $40,000 in another product? Those are all questions you will eventually need to think about.

Payment Terms

The usual way payments are made 30% before production and 70% before shipping (and after inspection). You don't necessarily HAVE to abide by those terms. It can be harder in the beginning to negotiate, but we've done many different payment types over the years:
- 30%/20%/50% (30% before production / 20% before shipment / 50% on reception)
- 50%/50% (50% before production / 50% on reception)
- 20%/80%
- 0%/100% (this is hard to get a factory to agree to though
- Monthly terms

- 100% after 30 days

The last three are extremely hard to get in the beginning. The rest are all feasible. Although some seem a LOT better than others, you can try to negotiate the terms you want (based on your Cash Flow needs) with your supplier. Sometimes you have to be creative to get the terms you want. It will depend on your situation/products. Keep in mind (and remind it to your supplier) that if YOU succeed and make more money, so do THEY. You can tell them that to grow faster, and for both of you to make more money, you would need X. Remember that you can't just take away from them. If you keep asking too much of them and not giving anything in return, you will not build a great long-term relationship with one of your most valuable assets.

General Tips

- Get your shipment inspected. It's worth to pay $100-300 to avoid the big issues that shouldn't have gone through in the first place. This is especially important for your first order. We have an employee full time in China that does Quality Control. That's how important you want it to be to your business. We didn't start that way though, so you'll have time to build up to that.
- Invest time in learning EVERYTHING about the products you are sourcing. This can be crucial! This is done in many ways:
    - Search on google; there are usually great forums that will help you learn more about the technicalities of your products.
    - Ask the suppliers more specific questions. Don't be afraid to look stupid.

- Call your competitors and ask them a question about their products (without revealing the true nature of your inquiry)
- This is so important because the more you are curious about the product, the more opportunities you can spot that people haven't before. It's why you don't need to be an expert in any niche you start in. You can do things that no one else did before because they didn't think it could be done a certain way. An example is you could end up using a different material for your products than everyone else because no one thought that using the new material would improve the flexibility of the product (you get the point).
- With the tactic I gave you to find quality suppliers, this should not be as much an issue but consider the following 5 factors when sourcing:
  - Price – Not at all cost though! Like I said before, don't try to drop the price too low or you'll end up with a shitty product
  - Quality – Goes without saying but it's better to pay a little more to ensure you have higher quality product.
  - Production Time – This is how long it'll take for your supplier to produce your order. It's very important, as it will impact your inventory management.
  - MOQ (Minimum Order Quantity) – The higher your order, the lower you will pay per unit. This is due to your supplier's material price.

- o Communication – Do not underrate this. It's important that your suppliers answer quickly and with a decent grasp of English. It can also mean that they have a bigger operation going.
- Try ALWAYS to have a backup supplier. It's easier said than done, but you never know what will happen to your current supplier. It's best if you can, within a reasonable time frame, have the other supplier produce the order for you.
- It's ALWAYS better to visit your supplier. I don't think anyone will be surprised by that one. If you can find cheap travel deals, it's worth it. Usually, you will be able to deduct it as a business expense as well (please consult with a professional before doing this). Attending the fairs can also be worth it to get new ideas and see products that you wouldn't be able to find otherwise. I would wait until you launched a few products before going unless you already live close to China.

Packaging

When you're talking with your supplier regarding packaging, you must ask them for a .ai file. You will be able to give this file to your designer so that he can take care of the design of your package.

If you're selling a set (multiple units of the same product), Amazon requires you to have to items sealed together so that they cannot be separated and are clearly labeled as a set.

Poly bags – what you need to know if you use them:

- Poly bags with a 5" opening or larger (measured when flat) are required to have a suffocation warning, either printed on the bag itself or attached as a label. You can verify Amazon's website for the exact wording of this label.
- Poly bags must be completely sealed.
- Poly bags or shrink wrap must not protrude more than 3" past the dimensions of the product. It could influence your FBA fees if it makes your product larger since they will calculate by measuring the packaging.
- Poly bags can be used to keep items together as a set.

Made in China
- Goods that are imported in the US are required to have a country of origin marking (such as the country of manufacture or production) of any foreign origin entering the US.
- What you can do is write "Made in PRC" or "Made in P.R.C." instead. It stands for "People's Republic of China." It makes it seem of better quality since most people don't know what it means and usually assume that China = bad quality.
- You can also write "Designed in XYZ Country" on the front of your packaging and still have the "Made in PRC" under your code bar at the back of your packaging. If you live in the United States, you could technically be "designing" the product in the US.

Logo
- Add your logo on your packaging, on your product, in your product inserts.

- This will help prevent people from hijacking your listing as you will have additional differentiation.

Reduce the possibility of breaking
- Always think of the customer experience. You're better off paying 10cents more for a sturdier packaging. This will reduce the possibility of having your packaging and product damage while it's handled by Amazon or your customer.
- If your customer receives a broken package, it will create a negative experience for them. Usually, that means a negative view of your brand and can lead to a bad review on your listing.
- You can speak with your supplier directly about your concerns. They should be able to help you ensure the quality of your packaging. (This is one reason why you request different packaging samples at the same time as your product).
- You can also ask them to do a drop them. Ask them to drop the package from approximately 3 feet high 4-6 times and inspect the packaging and product inside to see if it did any damage.

Label
- I recommend always printing an FNSKU label on your packaging.
- It will be exclusive to Amazon and unique to the seller.
- It'll be easier for you to prove if there is a hijacker on your listing as the FNSKU will not be the same.

Purchase Invoice (PI)

This is a contract between you and your supplier. Make sure it contains the following information:

- A detailed description of the product
- Photos
- Price
- Unit quantity (units vs. sets vs. pieces)
- Dimensions and weight
- Lead Time (Having a finish date – it's optional but nice to have)
- Payment Terms (30% deposit and 70% balance is standard)
- Company Stamp

While you're finishing up the invoicing, I recommend that you ask you're the supplier for 2 additional units. Tell them to ship those units as soon as they are completely (along with the packaging) to your photographer so that your photos can't be taken while the rest of your inventory is being finished.

Chapter 4 - Shipping

Now it's time to get your products shipped to their destination! There are a few things you should know right off the bat:

- Always make sure that the cost of customs clearance is included in a freight company's door-to-door service before placing orders overseas.
- Always get a quote in WRITING and make sure that is DDP (delivered duty paid). This means that the seller (not you) has to bear the risks and costs, including duties, taxes and other charges of delivering the goods to it, cleared for importation.
- Ask your supplier for a freight quote. Sometimes they have great relationships and could save you money on your shipments.
- Sometimes it's worth it to send about 20% of your shipment by Air Freight and the remaining 80% by Sea. This way, you don't pay that much more, you get your stock in much faster. This is great to do when:
  - You want to get started sooner; or
  - You're running out of stock, and you must receive it as soon as possible, or you will be out of stock for a long period.
- You must be certain that **all information supplied to the broker, air courier, or postal service is true and correct**. A power of attorney does not extend beyond their role as your Customs Broker. This is one rule you must learn. You are legally responsible for the facts declared in any declaration lodged for clearance purposes. Even if your broker makes an error, you are legally

responsible. One area that few consider in this respect is declared value. It is almost universal practice for Asian suppliers to under-declare the shipment value, or declare the goods as a gift, thinking they are doing you a favor. Chinese suppliers will do it routinely unless at the time of placing the order you firmly tell them not to. The majority of importers insist on them showing false values.

- You don't need to ship the product to you before shipping it to Amazon. We prefer shipping direct. Don't think for a second that your supplier doesn't know that your selling on Amazon and that they can't find your exact listing.

Basics of Shipping

Air shipping vs. Sea
- Air Shipping is usually split into
  - Air Freight – 15-20 days (door to door)
    - More expensive than sea freight
    - Dimensions and weight determine the price
    - Packing type is through cartons or palletized
    - Price will vary more than by sea depending on the period
    - Longer transit times (layovers) is usually cheaper than shorter transit times

  - Express – 3 to 5 days (DHL, FedEx, UPS, etc...)
    - Mostly used for samples

- Sea
  - Good for Oversized Products or Bigger Orders
  - Will take 35-45 days
  - Price is determined by dimensions/Volume (CBM – Cubic Meters)
  - Packing type is LCL (Less than Container Load or Consolidation) / FCL (Full Container Load)
    - LCL
      - Best use for below 15cbm shipments
      - You'll share a container with others (sharing the fee)
      - More expensive vs. FCL
    - FCL
      - Different sizes to choose from
      - Safer if all the container goes to the same location

The Larger a product is, the more economical it will be to ship by sea. If it's very small, it may be cheaper to send through Air!

How/When to use Air shipments?
- Launching a new product and you want to get feedback faster (send 30% by air, and 70% by sea can be an option depending on a case by case basis)
- Air shipments are usually better than running out of inventory (a % by air and the rest by sea works as well in this case)

Using Sea shipments
- Extremely cost effective for larger and heavier shipments
- Longer transit time (usually about 40 days from start to end)
  - About 15-20 days from port to port (China to LA) without the customs clearance

Better Management
- If you're shipping products from multiple suppliers, try to consolidate all the products using your freight forwarder. This will improve your margins and save you time managing the shipments.
- Plan and be on the lookout for Chinese holidays
  - Prepare your production accordingly so you can save money on shipping. Shipping during high seasons will cost you more.
- Most of the time, try to avoid DHL, UPS, and FedEx – their cost will be much higher. Use a freight forward or check out the in the "Getting Quotes" section.
- Learn how to calculate your shipment's cbm (cbmcalculator.com)

Evaluating different freight services for cost-effectiveness

Here I should add a note about cost-effectiveness because it can be too easy to think that the lowest freight cost per item is the one to choose. It may be, but that is not necessarily so.

You should consider what is known as opportunity cost. Faster delivery means a quicker turnover of your capital, and can considerably reduce your capital cost. While I am not teaching business economics, I suggest you consider what it might cost you in lost earnings on the capital needed to pay for your goods while they are in transit. It may cost you interest payments, or it may lose interest that you could otherwise earn.

There is also the need to consider the lost sales and ranking that might result from the delay.

FBA Shipping Labels

Carton Labels
- They are FBA labels applied to the master carton.
- You will receive this label while you're creating your shipment plan in Seller Central.
- Use this link if you're unsure how to create the shipping plan, check out the book resources at http://pixelfy.me/BookResources
- Make sure that your Packing Type is "Case-packed products."
- If you're sending in a product with 2 different colors, you'll have to make sure that you don't mix any of the colors. If you fit 25 units in a carton and you're sending 500 units (250 blue and 250 red), you will need to have 10 cartons with 25 units of red and 10 cartons with 25 units of blue.
- Decide WHERE you want those cartons shipped. To your home, warehouse, directly to Amazon?
    - There are pros and cons to all those methods. If you don't ship to Amazon directly, then you're spending more time

and money to inspect and ship the products again.

- Those labels are only valid for 3 months. Send them right before the inspection or 1-2 weeks before the final production date.

Inspections

Getting your shipments inspected is a no-brainer. It's not that expensive and it can be the difference between thousands of dollars lost and the quality you were expecting. Is it the last line of defense (if you're shipping directly to Amazon) before your customers receive the product. You must do it before paying the 70% balance!

Most people don't want to pay for the inspection, here are a few reasons why you must do it:

- It's way cheaper and easier to fix the issue before you paid the remaining 70% balance to your supplier.
- Once you've received the product in EU or US, it's usually too late to do anything about it (in most cases).
- Some suppliers don't want the inspection company to visit their factories (big red flag)
- Freight can be quite expensive, so better make sure that the product is perfect before.
- They will replace the products that don't pass the inspection.

What should they look for?

- The inspection companies know the drill. Nonetheless, you should confirm with them exactly what they'll do before. You'll want them to do:

- ○ Carton drop test – 5 times at 3 feet high
- ○ Unit drop test – 2-3 feet high drop
- ○ Check your competitors' complaints list so that they can test against those key points
- ○ Verification of quantity, item weight, dimensions, packaging (printing, sturdiness), labels, made in China/PRC marking

Here is a list of the companies that I consider to be reliable:
- Bureau Veritas
- TUV Rheinland
- SGS
- Intertek
- Sinotrust
- KRT Audit Corporation (US based)
- Cotecna
- Topwin (Chinese service cheaper than others)
  - ○ Contact them at safeimporting@topwin.com

I've also heard a lot of great thing about this service: https://www.guidedimports.com/services/quality-inspection/

Getting Quotes

What information you need:
- Carton Size
- # of Cartons
- Gross Weight of shipment or per Carton

- Address of the warehouse where your product is (if shipping FOB)**
- Which port (if shipping FOB)**
- Make sure that the duty rate is included (and is the same in all your quotes so that you can compare them)

**Not necessary if you use to pay your freight through your supplier

I suggest you get a quote for both Sea and Air Freight so that you can compare the difference in pricing. Sometimes you could be surprised. Depending on the weight and size of your product, it will vary a lot.

Where to go to find your Quotes?
- https://www.flexport.com/
- https://freightos.com
- Ask your supplier
- Shop around, they are so many different freight forwarders out there

Both websites above are quite easy to use. You should be able to look at YouTube or directly contact them if you need help.

Inventory Management System

Having a system in place to ensure you don't run out of stock and have too much product on hand is crucial. First, you have to know:
- How many units per day on average you're selling (ASV – Average Sales Velocity)

- We focus on the last 30 days, but will also look at the last 7 and 14 days to ensure it's still in line.
- You must always be able to answer "**How many days of inventory do I have left?**"
    - Also known as "Days on Hand."
    - It will be easily calculated: (Inventory on Amazon for product X / ASV of product X)
- **When will you need to reorder?** You must know your lead time
    - Lead time = Manufacturing time + Inspection time + Shipping Time
    - Reorder Time = Days on Hand – Lead Time – Safety Margin (14 Days)
    - The Safety Margin is there to minimize the risk of running out of stock
- **How much will you need to order?**
    - During Q4 (November – December will usually be 2-3x your regular ASV!)
        - It varies by category, but it will increase.
    - Reorder Quantity = ASV * 60-90 days
        - We like to order between 60 to 90 days of inventory per order.
    - You can also ask your manufacturer to hold onto 30-45 days of inventory in case you need to send in stock faster than you think. This will also save you storage fees.

Chapter 5 - CREATIVE WORK

Designing your brand – Logo + Packaging

Depending on which direction you chose to go for your products, your choices will be different here. If you decided to go ahead and build a brand, you would build a Creative Brief for your brand. I've included an example of what it should look like in the Annex. You will send this you the designer that you choose. For jobs like this, I recommend using a website like:

- https://99designs.com/
- https://www.designcrowd.com/
- https://www.fiverr.com

Make a few google searches before purchasing any packages on those websites. There are always coupons and discounts available to save a few $.

Photography

When you're getting your photos done, there are a few requirements you should anticipate:

- You should have already done your research on your competitors and how you can better differentiate yourself. This is the time to use it. (see Extra Tips below)
- I suggest that you get between 10-13 images. Get 2 images that you would consider your main ones.

This way, you can do some A/B testing later (will be covered later).

- Get at least 1 lifestyle picture of someone in your target market using the product. In those pictures, you can also emphasize the problem that it's solving.

- Get at least 1 infographic. You'll want to emphasize the key benefits of your products. You can also have an infographic that shows your product on the left and a generic version of your product on the right (never include your competitors' images). Under the images, you can compare with checks or Xs what your product has/does that the other doesn't. This is a great way to convince potential customers.

- **Before sending all the instructions to your photographer or designer to finalize your pictures, make sure you read the Chapter on listing optimization. I will cover how to better differentiate yourself, especially with your main image.**

Sample Creative Direction for Garlic Press

Image of garlic press with press facing towards the camera like this:

Image of garlic press inside box packaging like this

Image of garlic press spread apart laying on the table like this

Image of garlic press pushing out garlic facing camera like this

Works Great For Mincing Ginger Too!

Close up an image of garlic press with garlic inside pre-press like this

Large Chamber to Fit Any Clove

Image of garlic press + bundle garlic peeler like this

Extra Tips: When working with a photographer in person or online, it's very important that you give AS MUCH instruction as possible so that they get the images right the first time.

I like to find examples from my competitors and include them as direct links so that the photographer knows exactly what I'm shooting for. **Don't rely on the photographer to research to find out how to separate yourself from the competition, that's your job.** Putting in the time to provide detailed instruction saves you both time and money.

Another KEY aspect that you must not forget. Photos are investments. If you want to save a few bucks on your photography, you WILL regret it. It is crucial that you get the most amazing pictures possible. It makes all the difference between an INCREDIBLE listing and a decent one. **DO NOT CHEAP OUT ON YOUR PICTURES.** I've done it for my first product, and I had to get pictures redone because I regretted how bad they were compared to what they should've been. It will end up costing you more because if you want to succeed, you will have to get them redone.

Product Inserts

You should always have a product insert. No matter what your product is. You don't have to overthink it. Use a basic outline like this:
- Logo at the top
- Attention grabber under the logo (Different color, arrows to the text)
- Tell them exactly what they get (What you get...)
  - Longer warranty, Exclusive discounts, Giveaways

- Tell them HOW to join
  - Include a custom URL that they can type easily. I recommend www.pixelfy.me so that you can customize your link for easy typing and create a target audience of people who bought your product and took time to go to that link
- Add the last part about "Is there something wrong with the product? Email us right now, and we'll take care of you" and add your email.
- You can also add things like QR codes (using pixelfy.me) or Messenger Codes with ManyChat
- You can use ManyChat's growth tools to create links that you will use to redirect people to different pages, etc... The opportunities are endless, be creative!

Your URL link should drive them to a page where they have to join your Facebook and email list to benefit from the "What you get" list.

The ultimate goal of this insert is to get more customers that you know are interested in your brand since they bought your product. I will talk about how you can use that list to get "unlimited" product reviews later and launch your products faster. Don't get too excited though, the method to get more reviews for your new and existing products is not TOS-approved. I still use it because it's pretty much untraceable.

Creative Brief

Creative Brief for "Your brand."

The scope of Work: (this is what you want to be done)

Logo for 'Your brand' Yoga Brand (let's assume you're creating a yoga brand)
Brand Guide (color scheme, fonts) (more information on what a brand guide is here: https://99designs.com/blog/logo-branding/how-to-create-a-brand-style-guide/ - It's not necessary, but if you want to build a real business and remain consistent with your brand image, it will help a lot)

Goal:

To build a raving online following interested in premium yoga products that are eco-friendly.

Potential Product Lines:

Write down a list of potential products you will want to launch.

Audience:

Describe in VERY specific detail who your brand (or product) is targeted to. Don't leave anything up to chance.

These people likely shop at:

Where else would those people shop? Where do they hand out?

Words to Describe Brand:

If you could use up to 10 words to describe your brand what would they be?

You'll also want to include pictures of logos, products, design styles that you want your brand to look like. The designer's work will be much easier they know exactly what direction you want to head in.

Chapter 6 - Listing Optimization

There are two major steps for the customers. You want them to choose your listing out of all the other choices on the search page. Once they've made that first choice, you want them to have all the information they need to purchase your products. To get them on your listings, people will first look at your pictures, then # of reviews (and star rating) and then read through your title. The review part will not be covered here, as it is a combination of product quality, customer service, and review funnels.

It is also important that you can determine what a great listing looks like. I like to look at the example of the brand Anker. They sell over 300 million per year only on Amazon. By looking at their title, bullet points, photos, description (Enhanced Brand Content), you see that they are emphasizing what the customers want to know. They take advantage of their photos incredibly well to show answer the questions that they know their customers are thinking of and the ones they know they haven't thought of yet. They are pre-emptively answering those questions so that the customers don't have any reason NOT to buy their product.

Make sure that your listing looks great on mobile. Over 50% of purchases are now made through mobile. It's simple. Craft your listing as you will see below and then look at it with your phone to see how it looks. You'll see exactly what your customers see. The title length is much shorter on mobile, so if you are to include something very important that they must see, put it in the first 80 characters.

Why are you not getting enough sales?

There are usually two reasons why a listing is not getting enough sales:
1. Not enough traffic; or
2. Not converting enough.

Both of those metrics can be found in your seller central. "Reports -> Business Reports -> Detail Page Sales and Traffic." If you're not getting enough traffic, it means one of those things:

- You aren't ranked high enough. You should send traffic to your listings using your audience (Facebook or email lists).
- You're not using your PPC adequately

The "optimal" conversion rate is... undefined. You want to have it as high as possible, but the standard will vary from market to market. You should aim for at least 15%. Everything that will be covered about listing optimization here is to increase your conversion rate. Once you know your listing is fully optimized, it's easier to focus on sending more traffic. You don't want to be spending too much money on traffic while it's not properly optimized because you know you're losing out on a lot of sales you shouldn't.

General Tips

1. Spend as much time as necessary for your listing to have everything it needs
2. Treat the Listing as a Sales Page – Title (keyword infused headline); Bullet points = Bullet points; Description = Sales letter - restate why they should buy, what they get & CTA (call-to-action)
3. Speak/write to ONE person – your BEST buyer. Imagine you're at a bar with a friend, they have a problem your product can solve, speak conversationally and with compassion
4. Make them anticipate the REGRET of NOT HAVING the solution your product delivers
5. Hit all their hot buttons – what do they need to hear? Look for patterns in competitors' reviews, outside forums, etc.
6. Use VAKOG (Visual, Auditory, Kinesthetic, then Olfactory & Gustatory if it's something that smells good/tastes good). Paint a vivid picture of how their life will change
7. Power Up & Intensify every word – The power of Language
8. Satisfy every reader – Conscious & Reptilian Subconscious
   o Skimmers – Written Tonal Markings – They're in a RUSH
     ▪ Use ALL caps or *word* for important benefits, features, hypnotic feature anchors, so they stop to learn more, read and buy
   o Deep readers – Touch Every hot button. The way to make sure they're making the right decision

9. Use the Most Powerful and Persuasive Words in Sales
    o You, Money, Save, Results, Health, Easy, Love, Discovery, Proven, New, Safety, Guarantee, Free, Yes, Fast, Why, How, Secrets, Sale, Now, Power, Announcing, Benefits, Solution
10. Desire -> Focused Action (buy me!) -> Showcase Outcome
    o Question to ask yourself:
        ▪ Does everything in your listing speak to their Desire?
        ▪ Do you propose that buying your solution (benefits/features) is the focused action they should take?
        ▪ Do you showcase how it helps them get the Outcome they desire? (transform their life in their mind using your product?)
11. Write in a conversational tone and evoke as much emotion as you can
12. You're not convincing your customer to buy; he has to convince himself. You're just making it easier for him

Images

Your images are crucial to your success. You don't want to save $100 or even $200 on your pictures if it means not getting the ABSOLUTE best possible images you can. It's that important. The 1st goal of your listing images is to pick the curiosity of the customers, so they click on your listing (another extremely important factor is the # reviews + rating). Once they're on your page, your images must answer by themselves ALL the questions your customers usually ask themselves when buying your type of product.

Guidelines
- Images must be at least 1000x1000 regarding resolution (I suggest at least 1500x1500+)
- Main Image
  - White background (crucial)
  - The product takes about 85% of the frame
  - No graphics allowed (I don't play by this rule, and I suggest you don't either). I will explain why I choose to go against this rule in this section.
- Secondary Images
  - Graphics, text and different backgrounds are allowed

Main Image
- It is, without a doubt, the most important image
- It will impact your Click-Through Rate (from the search results) and PPC
- Should clearly showcase your product
- This plays a major part in helping you differentiate yourself from the competition
- Have at least 2 different ones so that you can A/B test
  - An A/B test consists of changing ONLY 1 variable and seeing how it impacts the results. In this case, you would change your main image for 7 days and look at the impact it had on all your important metrics (CTR, CR, sales, PPC)
  - Or... use another method that's a lot easier that I'm outlining in details in the book

resources at
http://pixelfy.me/BookResources

Not technically within the Terms of Services, but using the following tactics on your main image can help increase your CTR by a lot:

- Include small arrows, any small icons that can catch the attention of your potential customers
- Be sure that is it somehow relevant to your listing though

Secondary Images
- Display up to 8 additional images
- Used to sell the product's ability to solve their problems/pain points
- Use instructional photos/infographics. Showcase how easy it is to use, clean, assemble, etc.
- Have 1-2 pictures of someone from your target market using the product as it's intended (lifestyle pictures). If your target market is 40-50 years old mom doing yoga, do use an adolescent guy or a 300 lbs bodybuilder in those images. It's obvious, but still.
- ANSWER ALL the questions that they have and the ones they haven't thought about. Don't give them the opportunity to look at other listings because they aren't sure if your product can do XYZ.

Here are some examples/questions you may want to use or consider for your pictures:

- Think of WHY your customers are buying the product in the first place. What pain points is it solving? What are the first things your customers are looking for or thinking about when purchasing

81

your type of product? SHOWCASE those points/answers in your images.

- Have an image that compares your product features to your competitors (without ever mentioning any brand name or their actual photos)
- The rest of your images should showcase your product in different angles or situations. It depends on what it is. One thing that stays true for all products is that ALL of your pictures should SCREAM quality.
- It can be a good spot to mention your warranty.
- Include dimensions, small badges to indicate certifications that your product might have.
- Close up of features, product patterns, of product
- Feature highlights
- Social Proof images (pull 5-star reviews from your listing and add pictures of random photos online, so it looks like this):

You can also get your photos done locally. This will usually be charged by the hour. You can get a LOT more images for your money and get the retouching done on only the best pictures that you want either by your photographer or someone else (see below) for much cheaper.

If you need additional work done on your images, you can find people for a few $ per images on www.Fiverr.com.

Keyword Research

You should checkout the videos in the book resource section at http://pixelfy.me/BookResources. I had a chat with Helium10's expert and we went through their tools and the best way to get the most important keywords for your listing!

The first step to go through when crafting a listing is to do your keyword research. It is a crucial aspect of your product rankings. If you don't rank for the keywords with the most searches, then it's no mystery why the product doesn't have as many sales as you expected.

Amazon A9 algorithm

Amazon wants successful products to rank higher for RELEVANT keywords. Amazon scores each listing against a specific keyword in a relevancy percentage (you can use www.seller.tools to check out your score).

What is indexed for the search engine
- Title (200-character limit)
- Bullets
- Product Description
- Enhanced Brand Content (EBC)
- Backend Search Terms

- Subject Matter Field (not always available depending on your category)

What is NOT indexed for the search engine
- Questions & Answers
- Reviews

When you do your keyword research, you must distinguish between your primary keywords and secondary keywords.

The primary keywords (usually 20 keywords maximum)
- The most important and relevant ones to your listing
- The ones with the most search volume
- Repeated throughout title + bullets + description

Secondary keywords
- Keywords that are either more specific or broader, less targeted, but still relevant
- Entered into your description, search terms & subject matter field (In the backend)

I do my keyword research with Helium10 (https://www.helium10.com/).
- It's usually pretty straightforward to find your MAIN keyword. For example, if you're selling a yoga mat, it will be "yoga mat." To get the exact search volume, you could use the MAGNET tool from Helium10, and you would also find all the other relevant and semi-relevant keywords related to "yoga mat." With this data, you'll be able to create both the Primary and Secondary keyword list.

- If you want ideas to find your main keyword, you can go on Amazon and start typing in the search bar as if you wanted to buy (make sure category is set as "All" on the left of the search bar) and the autocomplete feature will give you suggestions for the top keywords.

Competitors
- Using Helium10, I would find the top 3 best selling in this category and write down their ASIN. Using their ASINs into Cerebro, I would look if they're ranking for keywords that I didn't get from using the Magnet tool and add them if that's the case.
- Take all of the keywords you have from using both the tools and put them into one document.
- Make sure that you remove all duplicate (can be done with Frankenstein – helium10 tool)
- Divide your list into Primary and Secondary keywords

Once you have all the keywords, the "time-consuming" part begins. You will want to go through all the keywords that you found and make sure that they're relevant to your product. One by one. Remove the ones that aren't

You'll want to make sure that the most important keywords are in your title (200 characters maximum), and then in your bullet points, back-end search term field along with the "Subject Matter" field, and then your description. The objective is for you to rank for as many relevant keywords as possible to increase the number of eyeballs that will see your products every day.

This tool is a great free google chrome extension to verify whether you are indexed for your keywords and your rank for those keywords. Install it using this link: http://bit.do/KeywordRankingExtension. Another quick way to verify that you're indexed for the keywords you're targeting is searching directly on Amazon in "all" the following: "ASIN keyword." If your product appears, then it means you're indexed for that keyword. It's fast if you only need to verify 1 keyword. The extension is great to do it to verify all your keywords at once.

Title

Your title should contain the most important keywords. You are limited to 200 characters in the title; use it carefully. The first 80 characters have the most impact. I'm both for and against using your Brand name in your title. We use it in all our listings because our brand has a little more recognition and all our products have a name, so it makes sense to include both. Other than that, I would suggest you don't put it in your title and make sure that you have as many RELEVANT keywords in your title while keeping your title coherent. You can separate parts of your titles with a "–" instead of the regular dash "-." It does a better job at separating the listing title. This last part is more of a preference as some people will you "," or only spaces.

It's important to tell your traffic that YOU HAVE WHAT THEY WANT. Be truthful though, only put it in your title if it's true. Your title should make as much sense as possible while the customers are reading it. Some people will write headlines like this: "Longest Run Time Samsung Galaxy Note 4 Battery Replacement with Longest Lasting 500 Cycles Rechargeable with Grade A Samsung Note 4 Battery

Cells Prevent Overheating to Guarantee Extended Performance".

While it is a great headline that touches on pretty much everything you need, to me anyway, it feels really hard to read. I prefer to separate it in a few chunks with dashes, and I also like to include the main keyword first and separate it from the rest of the listing with a dash. So, this is not a perfect example, but if the main keyword were Samsung Galaxy Note 4 Battery, I would write the listing like this: "Samsung Galaxy Note 4 Battery – Longest Run Time – Replacement with Longest Lasting 500 Cycles – Rechargeable with Grade A Samsung Note 4 Battery Cells – Prevent Overheating to Guarantee Extended Performance".

You can include some of the features of your product in the title if they are keywords that people search for. Here are some other things you must consider:

- Do not repeat words; it will not help your rankings. Sometimes you will have to though so that your title remains readable.
- You can use an "emoji" at the beginning of your listing title. While it is not allowed in the TOS, you can use it and if you get a complaint, remove it. I sometimes use a star emoji to grab attention from the customers. **If you are scared about having your listings suspended, do not try it!**

Bullet Points

The bullet points are where you should showcase the BENEFITS of your products. Always use the highest converting bullet format so that you can draw their eyes to notice the benefits and the transformation your customer needs to see and experience before they buy. Use capital letters and *stars* to draw attention. Before crafting the listing, ask yourself what the problem this customer is trying to solve by purchasing my product (you should already know this, but think about it again) is. Point out that problem right away in the bullet point. An example would be:

- "STOP DASHING TO THE POWERPOINT: LONGEST LASTING 3220-mAh 3.85V Li-ion Battery Note 4 Battery with Grade A Cells Last 500+ Charging Cycles & RESTORES your Phone to LIKE-NEW PERFORMANCE."

Here are a sequence works for pretty much all listings:

- **Bullet Point #1**: TRANSFORMATIONAL BULLET POINT. Use words like "Imagine You" or "Picture You" to begin the sentence. Include your TWO TOP Long-Tail Keywords when possible.
- **Bullet Point #2**: "What's Also Cool is..." Bullet Point – This is where the second transformational bullet point belongs; where you describe how else this will change your customers' lives, and include at least 1 long-tail keyword.
- **Bullet Point #3**: Unlike/Differentiation Bullet Point – Talk about how your product is better, different. This is an IDEAL place to use a CLAIM NO CLAIM with a long-term keyword that begins with the word 'Best [product type].' "While we won't say this is the BEST 8X42 MONOCULAR on the market, customers rate it a solid 4.96, better than any of the competitions."
- **Bullet Point #4**: Combine any features that still need to be mentioned. This is the LEAST READ

bullet point and usually only used for informational purposes.

- **Bullet Point #5**: EVERYTHING YOU NEED IN A [PRODUCT TYPE KEYWORD] Plus OUR INDUSTRY LEADING 'LOVE IT OR 100% of YOUR MONEY BACK' GUARANTEE. You can also include the length of your guarantee if you offer a great one — THIS IS YOUR 2nd MOST IMPORTANT BULLET

Description

You should use your Description as a small sales page. Use HTML (bold) and Emoji's (✅ - checks for example. You'll want to mention the following points:

- Create a small story around your product. Make them feel the pain of not having your product by talking about something that happens all the time to the people that don't have your product (and the solution it provides). Then, make them feel the pleasure and how much easier their life will be once they are using your product. You can ask them questions within the title FRAMED in a way that the only logical answer to those questions is the one you want them to think of.
    - What is compelling about your story? Wife/husband duo? Charity?
- Tell them how much easier life is when they will be using your product. They have to imagine themselves using your product and feel that it will solve their needs.
- REPEAT BULLET POINT #1 and YOUR HEADLINE combined, in a conversational tone. (Remember, natural language converts far higher than specs)

- Recap the main features and benefits. Do not simply repeat the bullet points. Flesh out the details.
- If our product has a ton of specs, list them in order near the bottom. Don't just drop them there though, make sure that you have a transitional sentence like, "The XYZ Product Has Everything You Want in a [Product Type] and it's easy to see why customers love it with specs like [Post Specs]
- Next, rebuild trust by restating your money back guarantee and warranty terms (like you'd explain them to a friend!)
- Finally, end with sentences that include 2 top keywords, an add to cart call to action, and if possible, 'scarcity' like, "Don't wait until XYZ returns to back order again..."

A small tip is to use https://wordtohtml.net/ and design your description however you want it to look in the "word" side and then copy the "HTML" side and paste into your Amazon's backend description section.

Backend Keywords

Use them to include all the keywords that are relevant, but didn't quite fit in the title or bullet points. This is also a good place to put keyword variations that aren't suitable for visible integration, like colloquial synonyms or common misspellings of certain keywords.

Here are a few things to keep in mind:
- 250 character maximum
- Make sure the keyword phrases are maintained and not broken apart. Amazon is not smart enough

to combine the two, so it's important that you maintain the keywords phrases that you're targeting.

- Are the keywords that you're targeting relevant? Amazon now scores your listing against each keyword to determine relevancy.
- No commas in between the keywords, only space.
- Do not include pronouns, single letters, dashes, periods, commas

Subject Matter
- Take advantage of the subject matter field. You can use up to 50 characters per line
- This the section that Amazon does not filter out. That means you can use 'brand' names with no penalty... at least for now.
- EVERYTHING is indexed!
- Include: competitor brand names, holidays, relevant events, specific audiences

Product Pricing

This will be brief. There are many ways to determine to price. Once you have a stronger brand, it's easier to be priced above everyone else and still outsell them. For now, focus on making sure that your price is high enough to cover all of your fees as I've already covered. Keep in mind psychology when you are pricing. For example, 32.90 can feel almost the same as 34.90 because they're both over 30$ but under 35$. There is so much to it; you can look at this site https://www.nickkolenda.com/psychological-pricing-strategies/ if you're interested in learning more about the different tactics. Don't spend too much time on it though, the rest of this document is a little bit more important overall. After that, you should also test your pricing using A/B Testing. See below for more information.

Enhanced Brand Content

To have access to Enhanced Brand Content (EBC), you need to register for Brand Registry 2.0. For that, you must have a trademark on your brand name. Not a patent on your product, just a simple text trademark for your brand name. It can take quite a long time to get though. You can get one in Mexico and Amazon will still approve it. It also takes considerably less time to receive so that's worth checking out.

As for the actual EBC, it's great. It makes your listing look so much better and more professional. You get to add a LOT more content. More images (of all kind of sizes), you can compare your products to each other, you can talk about your brand. Overall, it gives you more space to get the customer reasons why you're the only logical choice for them.

The other cool aspect is the EBC Video. Not all categories have access to it. If you do, that makes a pretty big difference... so get a 30 seconds video created about your product on Fiverr and upload it there. Just do it! Be careful though, you can't put outside links in your videos or talk about warranties and a lot of other stupid stuff like that. So if you do that, Amazon will simply not accept your video and you will have to modify it!

Setting up Email Feedback Sequence

What is an Email Feedback Sequence? It is the emails that a customer receives after he has purchased a product. You can control exactly when you want to send those emails and what they will say. There are a lot of great software out there that will automate this whole process for you. This is not something you want to be done manually, especially not as you grow.

<u>Why is it necessary?</u>
Those emails have 3 purposes. The first one is to encourage positive product review. The second one is to prevent negative feedback. The third one is to get your customers to interact more with you and your brand.

One thing that you must keep in mind when doing this is the amount of email to send. You don't want to be sending more than 3 emails. You can usually get the desired results with 2 emails. Sometimes 3 is required. You also don't want to send them too early, too late or one right after the other. It sounds complicated, but it is not. Don't worry!

I've attached a simple Word document with a template. Some of your customers will find it annoying, but we get a lot of positive feedback from our customers when they receive it. We also print the same long email (the first one) that you will see in this document and put it in a very small envelope with our logo on it. People will be curious when they open your packaging, and they will read the letter. This is another way to deliver your message to your customers.

Tools:
Zonpages (www.zonpages.com) – I recommend this. It's much cheaper, has all the features you need and does not charge based on the number of emails you send. They also have a 1$ trial 30-day trial. You don't have anything to lose! FeedbackGenius (www.feedbackgenius.com) – It's a more premium tool. It looks nice and is a little bit easier to use. But it is much more expensive. Especially when you will grow. You will be charged based on the # of emails you send every month.

Interacting with your audience

The more opportunities you get to interact with your audience, the more opportunities you have to transform them into raving fans for your brand. Whenever someone reaches out to you because they have an issue with their product, do your best to amaze them with your fantastic customer support. Try to offer them a replacement (through a fulfillment order) instead of a refund. This way, there is still a possibility that they will leave a review and recommend your brand to their friends. Usually, when you give a refund to your customer (especially if this is the first experience they have with your brand), you essentially terminate the relationship. It's very rare that a customer who has had a bad experience with the company will reorder (even if they got a refund). When you send them a new product, you give them the opportunity to keep using your products and hopefully have them come back for more.

A/B Testing and its role in your success

Would you like to sell more units at a higher price point? Well, you will never know if you can unless you try it. A/B testing is a way to compare two versions of a single variable, typically by testing a subject's response to variant A against variant B, and determining which of the two variants is more effective.

Here are some of the tools you can use:
- https://www.listing-dojo.com (free)
- https://cashcowpro.com/ (included in their subscription)
- https://splitly.com/

The purpose of A/B testing is to test (in this case, throughout 7 days for each variation) how well the variation you chose performs. You should only test 1 variation at a time. By variation, I mean either of those things: Title, Price, Main Image, Bullet Points, Description. Sometimes, the results are very surprising. Small changes can make a bigger difference than we expect.

The other way to "A/B" test is included in the book resources section. It's a lot easier and faster to do and get the results!

Chapter 7 - Building Your Brand

Before we get down to business... Let me ask you a question. It is definitely biased... But it's to prove a a point! What would you prefer to do in the future when you launch your products?

- Pay $350+ for a launch service and offer 100s of products at 90% off; or
- Pre-build an audience while you're sourcing your product and are waiting for the shipment to arrive at an Amazon warehouse and get your audience to buy at full price (or with a minor discount) by sending them the link in an email and/or on your Facebook page.

If you want to build a sustainable business with exponential growth, you probably chose the 2nd option. We'll go over how to build that foundation in this module.

Simply put, the goal here is to have an audience to launch your products. It can be on Facebook, other social media platforms, or even use other people's audience. You want to use any downtime you have (waiting for supplier's answers, waiting for samples, and waiting for your inventory to be finished and sent to Amazon). This gives you a window of about 60 days to work hard and make sure you are the in the best possible spot to get as many sales you can within the first few days of your product going live on Amazon. If you can only focus on ONE thing, work on your Facebook Page. The rest, in order of importance (in my opinion), are:

- Email list – through landing pages
- Product Inserts
- Website
- Instagram *(will not be covered, as I haven't used it enough)*
- Pinterest *(will not be covered, as I haven't used it enough)*
- Twitter *(will not be covered, as I haven't used it enough)*

One of the key things you have to keep in mind going forward is that you should always experiment. Remember that **there is not only one way for you to succeed**. If you look around, a lot of companies are doing amazing things. While they cover the basics regarding the quality product, customer service, etc. They have their own identity, they are different, and they embrace it. I will not go through any tactics step by step for multiple reasons:

- The specific tactics change extremely fast on Social Media. The general concepts don't.
- Most of the resources I will refer to all have detailed guides on their website on how to use them. Be resourceful!
- Social Media is the only aspect of the Amazon business where I wouldn't consider myself an expert. I haven't personally tried everything below. I've tried half and learned about the other half through friends that are doing it.

Your goal should be to have at least 1,000 followers on Facebook before your product does live on Amazon. It may seem like a huge and daunting task to accomplish, but it's not that bad. There are a few ways you can jumpstart your audience (Facebook page). The first one is through your friends and family. Someone of them may even be genuinely interested in the niche you are targeting. Have them like your page, so it has higher social proof when other people start to find your page. No one will like a page if has only 1-3 likes. Other ways you can get potential customers to like your page is through:

- Niche-related forums – google "forum ABC" where ABC would be a different way of finding your product or niche)
- Local groups focused or related to what you're selling (both online and offline)
- Reddit – find related subreddits where you can interact with people who are interested in your niche. This is great because you will learn more directly from your customers. How they're talking, what expressions they're using to describe their problems, etc. You can also end up privately contacting some of them on Reddit directly to get reviews for your product. Depending on what the rules of this subreddit are, you can contact the moderators to be sure but you can sometimes self-promote your page.
- Other Facebook groups. It's surprising how often you can join a (public or closed) group and participate a little bit in the conversation. After a few days or a week, you can contact the group's admin. A lot of those groups are not created with the purpose of selling something, so they won't have anything to lose by letting you post about your page or group directly in their group. You can offer them something in return before asking.

Another way to get people to buy your product for the first few days of your launch is through charity. This usually won't make your list bigger, but it can be a cool creative way to get a lot of people to buy your products. It's quite simple. Find a charity that revolves around (doesn't have to, but why not) with your niche. Send an email to the people in charge and tell them you would like to offer your product to their list. All the profits from the products that you would sell through their members would go back directly to the charity. Doesn't always work, but it's still a cool way to do something great and help boost your ranking for your launch.

I don't know your audience as well as you do (I hope!). You should know what kind of person they are, what they like, who they hang out with, etc. Use that knowledge to craft content on your page that will be appealing to them. Your goal is that they will impatiently wait for you to post new content every time because it will be interesting, intriguing, provide great value, and make them feel understood and important. In life, people want to be surrounded by people that make them feel better when they're around them. You can apply this concept to a certain degree with your social media.

Facts Tell, Stories Sell

We often try to sell by telling facts. While that's important to some degree, people buy with their emotions. If you want to build a brand, you must have stories around it. It shouldn't take more than 2-3 minutes to tell. The framework is relatively simple. You can modify it, so it fits your business.

1. You've (or your family, etc.) had this problem for a long time.
2. You've tried all the different alternatives, but nothing truly made a difference. It was starting to affect your quality of life deeply.
3. You've spent months/years trying to come up with a solution.
4. Finally, you found an amazing way to solve that issue. That solution is your product. Speak about all the fantastic benefits and the wonderful difference it made since you've started using it.

Interact with your audience

This is just a basic tip that's important for all platform. It's obvious, but it still needed to be said because it's really important if you want to grow through word of mouth exponentially. Create a connection, INVEST time speaking to them, engage your audience with questions, articles, cool stuff. Answer all of the comments, even if it's just to say things like "That's great!", "Thanks, we're glad you liked it" … We all like when people of "authority" acknowledge us.

Facebook

Some basics you should know before:
- Brand Page Dimensions:
  https://www.facebook.com/PagesSizesDimensions/
- Find content to share/post on your page when you create it, and they keep posting at least once a day. Here are some tools to use:

- o https://octosuite.com/ (discover "proven" viral content)
- o https://www.canva.com/ - Use to create Ads design, Cover Pages, etc....
    - ▪ https://www.Fiverr.com – If you want to find someone to do those things for you or cheap instead
- o Messenger Bots (I recommend ManyChat - https://manychat.com)
- General Tips
    - o Interact with your Fans
    - o Promote, Promote, Promote
    - o Ask them questions
    - o Share contents from other pages that you think may be interesting for your audience
    - o Hold a contest
    - o Run a poll
- When you start – post 3 videos that will go viral using octosuite... easier said than done!
- Provide Value, Life experiences, Images, quotes, funny pictures, videos

Advantages of FB Groups
- They will grow organically. After about 6 weeks or so FB will start sending you group members
- People in the Group can provide the content, so it makes it easier to manage
- Groups are more intimate. You will be a cult when posting and commenting in a group. People will get to know you.

Disadvantages of FB Groups
- Groups do not have the REACH of Fan Pages

- You cannot advertise "with" a group (But you can advertise with your page and link your group)
- It's harder to sell something in a group. Not because you are selling, but because your post gets pushed down

Advantages of FB Pages
- You get more reach. You should aim for 2x group reach per week. 8x per month
- You can boost posts and run ads!
- Using ManyChat – Build a list through the Fan Page

Disadvantages of FB Pages
- Not as intimate
- Won't get the CRAZY "Tribe" like groups

Best Practices
- Name your pages based on a Community
  - "I Love Yoga," "Yoga lovers."
- People DO NOT care about your BRAND here; they care about their interest. Make it about THEM. This is controversial advice. A lot of people will say the contrary. That you should include your brand name as the page name.
  - In the short term, it's easier to use a generic name, but it's better in the long term to have your brand name (*you can change the page name later as well*)
- Make it something that they are passionate about
- Then you become the leader for that group and passion
- Then that FEEDS into your BRAND
- Social Media is about ENGAGEMENT
  - Get their thoughts, opinions, comments

     o   Listen to people and acknowledge them

How to get more members / Start your group
- Creating a simple Engagement campaign – Something that would look like "Like cooking - Like our page."
- Have a PINNED post at the top of the FAN page to get them to join the GROUP
- Build a "COMMUNITY" inside your FB Group not a Brand
- If it is about an interest that you have, there is a good chance that many of your friends share this interest. Use them and your friends to get a jumpstart.
- Advertise your Group
  - Run Ad to a Page and link the group!
- Contests - This is great but DO NOT give away your product!! Give something complimentary (wait until you have MORE people!!!)
  - You could require them to Invite 10 people, and they would get access to it for free, or they would have to pay 197$ to have access
- As soon as people like your page, INVITE them to your group!!!!

ALWAYS ENGAGE!!
- FB rewards engagement
- Always comment, share, like comments, like posts, encourage others to do the same
- Posting and NOT responding is not good...
  - When you RESPOND, it gets the post BACK up!!

- Encourage people from your group to share by regularly reminding them of things like this: "If you see articles that you like, please share with the group!!"
- Reach out to people in the niche and get them in the group talking to your audience (they get exposure)

Website/Email List

How to BUILD the list?
- What PROBLEM does it solve?
  - Take that paint point and make my product the logical choice
  - Use a Squeeze Page for your product
- "People who have bought similar products in the last 30 days."
- SOLO Ads - Rent a spot in someone else's EMAIL list
  - Depending on the price and how targeted and relevant their audience is, this can be worth testing out.
- Contests for similar products
- Your Product insert should contain a link to a landing page and get the customers on your email list
- You can also create audiences from the customers that bought your product on Amazon (after the initial launch) and also create lookalike audiences to reach more potential customers. Either get them to like your page or send them to buy your products.

- I use Activecampaign, but if you want to use mailchimp (has a free plan), it works too

Once they are on your email list, you have to send them emails to convert them into paying customers. Here is something that I learn from a group that was in. **Do a quick hero's journey email** when someone subscribes on to your list then go STRAIGHT into 4-part series described below. You can see what the hero journey is here: https://en.wikipedia.org/wiki/Hero%27s_journey.   In short, you will describe your journey where you started with a certain problem, you went through different challenges, you thought of a solution (your product is the solution to the problem), and now you want to help people overcome the same struggles you had before. It can be a little bit more complicated, but it essentially boils down to this. IT DOESN'T HAVE TO BE 100% TRUE. You can bend reality to make it a lot more attractive than it is. You want your story to inspire, be compelling and make it, so people want to join your cause. **Facts tell stories to sell**!

<u>4 - Part Series (example I got from Daniel Ryan Moran)</u>
1. Story + Offer (REMAIL until they open - CHANGE THE TITLE)
   o Subject lines - "Think of paint point, the annoyance."
   o Must be tied to the story
   o NAME the offer around the story!
   o Only certain # available (scarcity)
     ▪ There are only 1000 left, the last year 2500 came, we'll post it to 200,000 subscribers later today... (use real numbers, don't lie...)
2. Reminder

- o Favorite/Special Use Highlight
- o We're doing X of these...
- o PS - in case you missed the original..." include the previous email

3. Deadline
   - o We've been inviting people to join. We want to help XYZ because ABC we're ending the promotion on a SPECIFIC DATE
     - ▪ Make sure you buy before SPECIFIC TIME
   - o PS - in case you missed the original..." include the previous email

4. Final Notice
   - o This is the last time you'll hear about XYZ Promo
   - o PS - in case you missed the original..." include the previous email

Monday - Tuesday - Thursday - Friday (do this whole 4-part series in maximum 7 days)

The HANDRAISE
- Customer Service is one of the highest converting mechanism
- Get them to write to you
  - o "Kill them with kindness ;)"
- Always invite them to send you messages "Write to us."
- Always go for the SMALLEST YES POSSIBLE
  - o An example would be a Squeeze page with "WOULD YOU LIKE THIS FREE XYZ?"

ManyChat

ManyChat is a Facebook Messenger Bot. Simply put, this is a service that you get can for free or pay $10 a month to automate a lot of tasks for you on Facebook. You can automate customer interactions, create a small store within your messenger chat, you can also make it, so it messages everyone that comments a particular word or phrase in a post or an ad on your page. They will be added to your messenger bot list.

Why is this so "in" right now? People have an almost 90% open rate on their FB messages, which is insanely high. They CTR (click-through rate) for the links that you would include in such messages is also extremely high.

Getting people on your ManyChat list by posting something like this:
- "We're thinking about releasing this, WOULD YOU WANT THIS?"
- "Hey we've got a new VIP list that gives you front of the line access/first dibs to XYZ, would you want in?" Then comment "yes," and we'll add you

Another great usage of Messenger bots is to get MORE reviews. You can use it in concert with ZonPages to accomplish this (by targeting the people who already bought from you) or by simply posting in your FB page without doing an Ad. The principle is quite simple:
- Post on your FB Page is saying that everyone who has bought from you on Amazon can XYZ if they comment "whatever comment you set it to" on the post.
- In this context, XYZ can be:

- o Win an Amazon gift certificate;
- o Get a 20% coupon off your new product;
- o Get a Starbucks gift card
- o You get the point. Make it enticing enough so that it's worth the few seconds of "effort" they will have to go through to comment on the Post and then provide you with their Amazon Order ID.
- Ultimately, you tell them that they will need to leave a review to be entered in your giveaway (ONLY SAY THIS PRIVATELY, NEVER IN YOUR PAGE FOR EVERYONE TO SEE)
- A "better" way to do it would be to simply post on your page and say "If you've purchased from us before and LEFT A REVIEW, comment "......" and we'll reach out to give you a surprise (or enter them in a giveaway). This way, you don't ASK them to leave a review. If they bought from you and didn't leave a review, they will tend to go back and leave a review just to be included in your little competition.

*This is a pretty basic overview. I didn't want to go too deep into details as things change very fast and it's better for you to try it out... or **join my Facebook Group** http://pixelfy.me/FBGroup to ask me specific questions!*

General tips
- Be creative – This applies to EVERYTHING in your business, not just this particular section. This advice is vague, but still so important. Out of the box solutions or products can help you save or make a lot more money both in the short and long term.

- Here are some tips for Pattern Interrupting (Don't use all of these, you can test them if it makes sense to incorporate them in your ads or emails but don't go out of your way to add them in, or it won't look very natural). I also want to emphasize that these are not tools to use to grow your business. I would only use some of those tactics to get a kick-start. Ultimately, that is entirely up to you.
    - Warning/Danger signs everywhere on your ad
    - Humans recognize faces (face swap something WEIRD to grab attention right away)
    - Mess with the FAMILIAR, but make it feel WRONG
    - Use OPEN LOOP (An unanswered story will make people we want to know how it ends)
    - "This tea bag is the secret to XYZ, but I'll get to why in a minute... But first, let me tell you a story."
    - LEAVE some mystery to make sure that they want to keep reading
    - Use GIF instead of images whenever you can
    - Give people a reason to STOP (people SPEED scroll)
    - Something OUT OF PLACE (we're OCD we notice things that are a little out of place)
    - Random Email Subject Lines (rnhnjdsnjsdREADTHISNOWf ///////////// RE: ....)
    - Use typos in your emails or subject line
    - Add borders with different colors

- Make something feel like it's blending and surprise them
- CONTROVERSY is a GREAT way to pattern interrupt
- CONTRAST of color
- A person with a facial expression of SHOCK (baby especially catches attention)
- "ENTER TO WIN" (written in color contrast)

You can use "fake" testimonials from stars (using www.cameo.com). This one is a little bit funny. You can pay a celebrity or athlete a pretty low amount to make them say pretty much anything they want. You could get them to say "XYZ brands are amazing, their products are fantastic" and use it in your ads. I haven't tried it, but some of my friends did some cool stuff with it! **Double-check before using in ads**.

Using Different tools to extract your Customers' data from Amazon

This will be useful to get more reviews and also launch products later on. You will need minimum 100 orders for it to work. But it starts to get more interesting with over 1,000 orders. You can extract your customers information (names and addresses) from SellerLegend or directly from Amazon.

Then, you can match the data you have on Amazon to their Facebook profiles through customer audience creation in a Facebook Ad and use your newly created Facebook audience to get them to like your page, to target them for your new product launches or to use that audience to create a lookalike audience (get that audience to like your page or buy your products as well).

Closing thoughts

I've given you a quick introduction. You don't have to apply everything. Social Media is something that takes time to master. You don't have to be a master to get good enough results to get going in the beginning. There are so many other things that you can do. I've seen people use Pinterest, Instagram, Twitter, Whatsapp, SMS, and plenty of other ways to reach their audiences.

I try to minimize my Social Media advertising. The cost of advertising keeps rising, and it's reducing the profit margins by quite a lot. The best way to grow this fast with almost no advertising spend is through word of mouth. People tend to surround themselves with other people that have the same interests as they do. If everything you do is great/amazing (not just good), they will tell their friends. We're so used to dealing with shitty products, customer service, warranties. Take time to look at the customer experience as a whole and make sure you can make it fantastic from the beginning to the end. I understand that being on Amazon limits what you can do, but it's still a great exercise to go through at least once.

As long as you're learning, you should be progressing in the right direction. If you're in it for the long term, your decision making will be much different than if you focus on only short-term wins. Keep it in mind!

Chapter 8 - Product Launch

Before you go through this module, read the Amazon Search Engine PDF if you haven't. One thing to keep in mind when doing a product launch is how CRUCIAL the first 7-10 days are. Amazon will give you a boost when you first launch a product. It'll be easier for you to rank during that period. As soon as your product goes live on Amazon, your listing should ALREADY have been optimized. You should ALREADY have your main pictures. You should have at least 5 people ready to buy the product and leave a review (see Reviews section for more information).

Another KEY point for your launch is Amazon PPC. You will launch your PPC after your first review. Use the technique I've outlined in a previous module. Once you get to 5-10 reviews (make sure to have a 4.3-star rating or more or else your CTR and CR will GREATLY suffer and impact your ranking abilities), you will want to turn on PPC HARD. I will cover exactly what to do with your PPC in the Advertising module. This combo of having minimum 5-10 reviews (20 is obviously better, but you can still start at around 10) with a minimum of 4.3-star rating then switching on PPC is often more than enough for you to rank your products very well.

This is extremely powerful because you're getting FULL priced sales instead of 90% off. Amazon takes them into account differently. The people buying your products through PPC are ACTUAL customers, not pieces of shit buying your product for 1$ then trying to hijack your listing.

Also, since they're full price sales by actual customers, they can leave a verified review (which they can't when buying with a 90% off discount), AND they can potentially buy your other products and recommend them to their friends. All of those factors add up.

If you're in a very competitive niche or if you want to overkill your launch, you can use both Hard Amazon PPC + Launch service (or FB ads with rebate) to launch to the first page very fast. I will cover how to set up your launch PPC in the Amazon Advertising Module.

If you've followed the previous lessons, you should have a Facebook audience and/or an email list built. This way, you won't have to give away your products at 90% off. You can still offer a small 10-20% discount to get people a little excited. Here's what you should keep in mind:

- Scarcity – Tell them that there are only 20 units available at that 20% reduced special launch price. Either through your Facebook Page (get them to contact you through Messenger with ManyChat) or with your email list. This way, if more than 20 people get in touch (which they should), you can give this "special" price to everyone who reached out.
- Hype – Talk about your products and show pictures to your audience before it's available. Tell them that it will solve their problems (be specific and use emotions).
- PPC – Start when you get your first review. Be aggressive. It's okay if you ACoS is over 100% when you start. See it as investing for Amazon's data. After 7 days, you will have sufficient data to analyze the reports and make decisions on what to

do next with your PPC. We'll cover that in greater details later.

How many units to giveaway?

If you're set on going the 90% off route, at least make sure that your listing is fully optimized. Don't think you're different and you can crush your competition by not doing everything right.

One way to do it is to contact ZonBlast. They're responsive, and you can send them your listing, and they will help you decide which keyword to go for, what length for your giveaway, and how many units to giveaway. You don't need to pay anything or use their service. Don't tell them you don't intend to use them (if that's the case).

If you want to do it yourself, you can use a tool like Helium10. You can you a reverse ASIN tool on your top competitors to confirm your main 2-3 keywords. Then, you can use Magnet or Cerebro again to figure out how many units you should give out over 8 days.

Both those alternatives are valid, as long as you start with 5-10 reviews, 4.3-star rating, a fully optimized listing, and hardcore PPC!

Another option you have if you're launching and getting full priced sales is using the same estimate from Helium10 but giving about 40-50% of that amount since full priced sales have a much bigger impact on Amazon algorithm.

Reviews

This is a very touchy subject! I will tell you a few compliant and non-compliant ways to acquire more reviews. It's up to you to evaluate the risk vs. the reward. Here are the main options to consider:

Automatic Email Sequences
I've already covered them and gave you 2 templates to use. This is a MUST.

Early Reviewer Program
(https://sellercentral.amazon.com/early-reviewer-program/program-overview)
I think this is a terrible option. It's free to enroll, and Amazon will incentivize people to buy your product by giving them a 3$ gift card to customers who purchase and leave a review on your enrolled products. The reason I think it is terrible are the following:

- It costs $60 – you will pay when you receive your first review through the ERP program. You can end up only getting 1 review as your enrollment will last for up to 1 year or when you get 5 reviews.
- No control – This is my biggest issue. If you start your product with anything else than a few 5 stars' reviews (and maybe 4 stars), you're shooting yourself in the foot. A product with less than 5 reviews and less than 4.3-star rating doesn't look good.

Friends & Family
This is the easiest way to get started. I don't recommend using your direct family or friends. It's better if you use friends of your family, friends of friends, or friends of your

friends' parents. You get the point. This is usually only used to get 3-5 reviews in the beginning. What you'd do is send them the full amount on PayPal (+5$ if you want to encourage after they left the review) and ask them to leave a 5-star review. You may want to ask for 1 4-star review, so it doesn't look too strange.

Facebook Groups

Don't use the Facebook review groups... your will have your products/account suspended. Don't use those groups. Just DON'T.

The alternative are groups or pages related to your product. Find them, reach out to people that are active in those privately (and without adding them to your friends list on Facebook) and tell them you want to get their feedback on your new product. You will send them the money first through PayPal and ask them to purchase directly on Amazon. You can include an Amazon URL using pixelfy.me to get some more ranking juice. Tell them to send you their feedback within a week on Facebook messenger. If it's positive, get them to leave it as a review!

Review Websites

I haven't been up to dates with those websites. An example would be www.Rebatekey.com. The idea of the website is you offer a rebate to the customer. The customer will buy the product on Amazon at full price and send you his Order ID through RebateKey's messaging system. You will end up paying (number of units your give away) x ($ amount off your product + 2.95$ per product). You will be able to message him directly on that private messaging system. You can ask them to give you a few reviews. The number of reviews you will end up getting per products given away is quite low. Unfortunately, people must get spammed in there too now so there aren't as responsive as they once were. You can try it and see, but it's not the best option.

Testing Group

In a previous module, I mentioned that you should build your email list through Packaging Inserts that get people on your email list. If you have a website, you should also have an email opt-in to gather more emails. The testing group is all done through email. You use people (most of the time) that have already purchased 1 product from you. You'll email your list and tell them that you have a private testing group that you use to get quick feedback on your new products. If they're interested, they should fill out a form. Create a Google form asking their email, name, PayPal email, and what product they're interested in (if you have more than 1 product you want feedback for). Then, you'll contact them through email, explaining to them that you will send them the price of the product + a small $ as a token of your appreciation. Finally, you tell them that they will have to review the product within a few days of reception AND to contact you if they have any issues before leaving a review. You can also include a small FAQ in your email telling that the reason you're making them purchase through Amazon rather than sending them directly is that you don't have a warehouse in the US or wherever you're located and therefore need to use the stock that is in Amazon. This works quite well if it makes a least a little bit sense for you to have "testers" for your products.

There are so many ways to get reviews. Use your creativity and figure out a way for you to get a few reviews as soon as possible when your product launches. Make sure to be extremely careful or remain TOS-compliant.

ManyChat Review Strategy

Check out the book's resources at
http://pixelfy.me/BookResources

Product Launch Strategy with RebateKey and Pixelfy.me

Check out the book's resources at:
http://pixelfy.me/BookResources

Amazon Giveaways

Amazon giveaways is an advertising tool that Amazon offers. You can use it differently to promote your products when you launch. To create an Amazon Giveaways, go on your Seller Central -> "Advertising" -> "Promotions" and then click on Giveaways. Select your product. You'll end up on another page.

1. Select the number of products you want to give away (3-4 is enough).
2. Enter your Brand name in Host Information and your Logo in Customer Image
3. Select "Lucky Number Instant Win" and 1,900.
4. Select "Watch a YouTube video" and enter your YouTube video link.
5. "Yes" to offer a discount to entrants. You will need to create a promotion with 10-20% off for your product, and every entrant will receive it. Which increases a little your exposure.

This is not a method that will get you 100s of sales. This is to see if you can get a few more sales. You can also create a short YouTube video about your product (can be cheap to do on Fiverr). You'll want to include links to your website and mention something about promotions if they signup for your email list and like your FB page directly in the YouTube Video description.

Chapter 9 - Amazon PPC

While this chapter will give you great insights into Amazon PPC, the basics and what you need to know over time to manage your campaigns, there is SO much more to it.

Auto Campaigns

Auto campaigns are directed by Amazon to match your products to the keyword they think will be the most relevant. After a week, you're able to use the data from Amazon to better optimize the campaigns yourself. You'll be able to update your listing if you find search terms in your PPC reports that are converting very well and improve your listing with that information. The better optimized your listing is, the easier it'll be for Amazon to find those relevant keywords for you.

Manual Campaigns

You are responsible for the entirety of the campaign. You will be required to input the keywords manually. You'll put in your Primary and Secondary keywords for the earlier module and also add more keywords that you will get from your auto campaign's search term report. This will allow you to target the keywords that convert well. You'll have a lot more control through keyword selection and the bid for those keywords. You can't adjust your bids for specific keywords in the Auto campaigns. By using the Manual one, you can bid higher for certain keywords if you want to be sure to be on the first page search results.

Campaign Structure

The structure of the PPC campaigns can be quite confusing when you're just starting. Here it is:

- Campaign Level
    - Ad Group Level
        - Ads Level

Campaign Level
Used to outlines products categories. It will help organize your campaign better. An example would be a campaign for the tables, a campaign for desks, a campaign for plates. You get the point. They also allow you to control the budget for your campaign. You will determine how much you're willing to spend daily.

Ad Group Level
It allows you to break the campaigns into further type of products. **Each Ad group shares the same set of keywords**. You can have multiple SKUs in each Ad Group. You also don't control the budget (it's only done at the campaign level). An example would be:

- Tables (Campaign Level)
    - Luxury Tables (Ad Group Level)
    - Plastic Tables (Ad Group Level)
- Plates (Campaign Level)
    - Plastic plates (Ad Group Level)
    - Ceramic plates (Ad Group Level)

You have to be careful though. Sometimes all of your budgets will go into luxury tables for example. Therefore, you won't get any impressions or click for plastic tables. Since you have no control over the budget, you'd have to separate them at the campaign level instead.

Ads Level
SKUs that you'll be advertising.

- Plates (Campaign Level)
  - Plastic plates (Ad Group Level)
    - Reusable plates
    - Non-Reusable plates

Since you share the same keywords for both Reusable plates and non-reusable plates, you could run into the same issue as I mentioned above for the budget. If one of your campaigns outperforms the other by a lot, then the other wouldn't get any impressions. Or it wouldn't have the best keywords for it. You'd need to separate again at the campaign level.

Alternatively, you go 1 Campaign per SKU. This way, you don't run into any of those issues anymore. It will allow for the best budget control. In the end, you'll run multiple different campaigns per SKU as you'll see below so it'll be very important to have a good naming convention.

Match Types

Match types are only used in manual campaigns. You can't use them in auto campaigns. Once you set up your Manual campaign, you will choose if your keywords match is:

- Broad

- Phrase
- Exact

Broad Match

This acts like a very wide net. It'll catch a lot more keywords.

- Any words can be added before, in the middle, or after your keyword phrase
- It also includes plurals and misspellings
- It is the cheapest, least relevant and least targeted option

Phrase Match

The phrase match is narrower than broad match.

- Your keyword phrases cannot be split/broken. Keywords can only be added before or after.
- It also includes misspellings and plurals/singulars
- More targeted and more expensive than broad match

Exact Match

It doesn't get any narrower!

- It will only target the keywords you're entering. They must match exactly
- Allows plurals, singulars & misspellings
- It is the most expensive and targeted option

Broad and Phrase Match Campaigns can be used to provide you with more keywords data. Looking at your search term reports, you'll be able to discover new keywords that convert very well. You can then add those keywords to your exact campaigns. Same with the auto campaigns. They provide you with a lot of potential keywords to use in your other campaigns.

ACoS

ACoS is the most important metric for your advertising on Amazon. It stands for Average Cost of Sale. It is determined by this formula (Ad Spend / Total Sales). For example, if it cost you 10$ in PPC to generate a 30$ sale, your ACoS would be 33%. It is a great measure to see very quickly how effective your campaigns are for your different SKUs.

What ACoS should you target? It depends on your margins and what phase of your PPC campaign you are in. In the launch phase, it's not that important. It can be 120%, and it will be fine. But one your launch phase is over and you switch to the Optimization phase; it's important to know if your campaigns are profitable or not. The way you'll determine it is quite easy. You'll take your Total Sale amount for your product and remove all of your expenses (except ad spend). This includes any tax, Amazon Fees, COGS + shipping, and other overhead you may have. You'll end up with your profit. If your profit is 25%, then your campaign will be profitable if it's under 25% because you will still have a % of profit left. If it's over 25%, then you're losing money on every PPC sale you make. It doesn't mean you should stop your campaign immediately. Since you're driving sales, you're helping your organic ranking and conversion rates, so it's still good. Unless you're stuck at 75%+ and you're trying to optimize your campaign, then you may want to consider pausing it at least. You'll see soon how to optimize your campaigns. The same concept applies to your overall account. If your total ACoS is 25%, but your overall margin is 35% for your account, then you're still up 10%.

When starting new campaigns, I recommend setting your bids slightly above the recommended amount.

PPC for your Launch

When setting up your launch PPC campaign, you should already have some PPC data. Since you'll be launching your product after getting about 15 reviews, you should already have started you PPC. You'll be able to use the PPC Optimization section below to manage your budget, your bids, harvest keywords, and remove your losers. Once you're sure that your listing is optimized, that it has 15 reviews+ and a 4.3-star rating+, you can increase your PPC budget to 200 daily. The goal here is that your ads don't run out of the budget. If you're unsure, you can gradually increase it. It'll be important that you look at your bid amount as well. But this is covered below!

**To make sure your listing is well optimized, go on seller central, click on:
Reports -> Business Reports, then By ASIN -> Detail Page Sales and Traffic by Parent Item.
Look at the column named "Unit Session Percentage." This is like the conversion rate, but it considers multiple units purchases as well. It should be very close to your conversion rate, especially if you don't have a lot of multi-units orders. If you're above 15%, you have a good conversion rate. It varies by category, but it is still a good baseline. If you can get over 20%, you'll be doing very well. You can also keep track of the number of sessions. If you're converting at about 20% and your number of sessions is very low, you can send outside target traffic through

influencers or Ads, or you can increase your spend or bid from Amazon PPC.

PPC Optimization

Campaign Budget Management

One key aspect is to manage your overall campaign management. It should be done as frequently as necessary. The goal is:

- Increasing the budget spend on the campaigns that are under your target ACoS to allow those successful campaigns to spend more money and continue to drive more profitable sales

When you're launching new campaigns or products, wait at least 3 days before increasing your budget. It's highly that your campaigns will run out of budget during those first few days. You want to give some time for the sales to come in. It's due to a 7 days advertising lag by Amazon. Amazon will send you an email when your campaign is out of the budget. They will also show it in the Campaign manager. They will give you a recommendation of how what you should increase your budget too.

Steps

- Go through all their notifications, one by one, and verify whether the ACoS is under or over your target ACoS. I like to check Month to date (MTD) data (especially if after the middle of the month.
- If it's OVER your target ACoS, let it continue for a few more days.
- If it's UNDER your target ACoS, increase it to an amount between what you're at now and their

recommended amount. You can gradually increase it over time, or increase it to their recommended amount right away. It's a matter of preference.

Keyword Mining (harvesting)

You'll go through your search term reports ONCE A WEEK to pull the data from your auto, broad, and phrase campaigns to create or update campaigns. As I said earlier, exact campaigns are not used to get new keyword data.

Go to Advertising -> Campaign Manager -> Advertising Reports
- Report type – Search Term
- Report Period – Last 30 days
- Download the Excel File

How to read this report?
- It's organized by campaign name, Ad Group, and keyword
  - The keyword is the one that you're using to bid for a specific search term
- Match type – Whether your campaign is Broad, Phrase, or exact
- Customer Search Term – what the customer found your product with (what search term they typed in the search bar)
- Impression - # of times your ad was shown
- 7 days' total sales & **7 days' total orders** (This is what we'll look at)

What you'll want to do to analyze the report is the following:
- Filter your data and remove "exact" by filtering through the "Match Type" column

- We'll then filter by column "7 Days Advertised SKU Units" to >0 (so only the ones that sold 1+)
  - This is important because those are the sales that you got directly through our advertised SKU. If someone clicks on your sponsored Ad from SKU1 and they end up buying SKU2, then you don't want to take it into account for the SKU1 data. That's where the "Advertised SKU" comes from in this case.
- Copy the filtered data into another spreadsheet to separate this data.
- Verify that the "Customer Search Term" is not the same as the "Keyword" since you're trying to look for new keywords. You can use formulas in excel to do it faster. If you're not sure how you can either google "compare 2 lists in excel" or use a tool like this http://www.molbiotools.com/listcompare.html that will give you back what keywords are present in both list. You can manually remove them after.
- Then, you want to remove duplicates from WITHIN the "Keyword" columns. This is even easier to do. Select all the data, create a pivot table and select only the Rows as keyword and you will get all the unique keywords.
- Copy the final list to a separate worksheet and verify if your new keywords are ALREADY in your exact campaigns. If they are, remove them.
- Then, you'll create a campaign with the same nomenclature. It'll be a broad campaign. You'll add all your keywords, set a daily budget and **add a default bid of 1.06$ for all your broad campaigns**. Then, apply suggested bid for the rest. Once that's

done, you'll repeat the process of creating campaigns to Exact and Phrase campaigns (separately).
- You'll want to add those same keywords as NEGATIVE keywords in your AUTO campaign as well. You'll need to click on your campaign, click on the tab "Negative Keywords" and add the same list of keywords as "Negative Exact" match type. This way, we'll continue to get new keywords.
- This is a process you'll repeat every week.

Keyword Bid Management

This is something you'll also do once a week. The purpose is to decrease the bids on your keywords that are over your target ACoS to reduce inefficient spend on those keywords. The goal is to decrease your ACoS and spend.

We'll use the following guidelines:
- If your ACoS > Target ACos
  o Decrease bid by 20%
  o if < 7 orders for the last 7 days for that keyword (lower volume keywords)
- If your ACoS > Target ACos
  o Decrease bid by 15%
  o if > 7 orders for the last 7 days for that keyword (higher volume keywords)

Go into Campaign Manager.
- Change the date rate to customized. Look at the last 7 days starting 2 days before the current date. If we're the 3rd of the month, your end date should be the 1st. The reason why is that it takes some time to update all this data from Amazon.

- Look at the campaigns that are above your target ACoS
- Click on it and verify that it's still the same time frame (sometimes it can change)
- Sort by spend (highest to lowest). Click on the Ad group.
- You can use the "filter" function that is near the "Create Keywords" button instead of using the Excel reports.
- Click on the filter, then on ACoS and filter for "greater than" your target ACoS and "Save"
- Add another filter "Orders" at "less than 7"
- Click on Select all (the little box on the top left) and Adjust ("Decrease bid by %" – 20%)
- Change your filter to "orders" greater than 7... and select all... adjust bid "Decrease bid by %" and enter 15%.
- This is an ongoing process and a very baseline way to easily manage your PPC

Removing the losers

Your losers are the keywords that have PPC clicks but 0 sales. This is also a weekly process that you'll go through. This way you'll try to maximize your budget. By doing this, you'll get to reduce your ACoS and also analyze what keywords are not converting. If they're keywords that you want to rank for, you'll have to ask yourself whether they're relevant to your listing or not. You'll have to look at your listing (title, bullets, etc.) to be sure it's in there.

We'll use the following criteria:
- 8-10 clicks or higher with – sales = Losers

- Use at least 7 days of data

Steps
- Go your Campaign Manager
- Use customized date (Look at the last 7 days starting 2 days before the current date).
- An easy way to find those keywords would be to extract a search term report and sort your columns by 8 or higher Clicks and 0 sales.
    - You can also stay on seller central and use the filters in the ad group you're targeting. Use filters "Clicks" > 8 and Orders = 0
- You'll want to pause the keyword immediately. Then, it's time to analyze whether you want to remove it (when you archive it, you can never get it back, if you pause it, you can activate it again later).
    - If it's not a keyword that is relevant to your listing, go ahead and delete it.
    - If it's relevant, go in your listing and figure out why it's not converting well.

Conclusion

It's time to fly now little birdie. I know it's overwhelming at first. There are a lot of things to consider when selling on Amazon. This book's only goal was to introduce you to Amazon and give you a solid foundation upon which you will build your own eCommerce empire.

Working with me

If you're interested in working with me, whether you're a new or advanced seller, I do have different options available. I work directly 1-on-1 with a few select clients, but that is a lot more expensive! If you want to dive deeper into my world and for us to get to know each other better, check out all my FREE stuff

YouTube Channel -> http://pixelfy.me/FBAYouTube
Facebook Group -> http://pixelfy.me/FBGroup
Instagram -> http://pixelfy.me/FBAInstagram
Website -> https:// FBAMavericks.com
Book Resources -> http://pixelfy.me/BookResources

If you're ready to jump in now and work with me directly, check out https://FBAMavericks.com/nextlevel

Made in the USA
Middletown, DE
17 September 2019